Civil Society
& Social Policy

Voluntarism in Ireland

Fred Powell
Donal Guerin

A. & A. Farmar

British Library Cataloguing in Publication Data
A CIP catalogue record for this book is available from the British Library

Typesetting and text layout by A & A Farmar
Printed and bound by **e-print** Limited.

A & A Farmar
Beech House
78 Ranelagh Village
Dublin 6
Ireland

ISBN 1 899047 36 0

CONTENTS

ACKNOWLEDGEMENTS 7

INTRODUCTION 9

1: CIVIL SOCIETY & SOCIAL SOLIDARITY.. 11

Philosophical origins and political issues 11

Postmodernity, society and individualism..................................... 16

Welfare, civil society and voluntary action 19

Public opinion, social engagement & active citizenship.................. 26

Conclusion.. 30

2: CIVIC VIRTUE, RIGHTS & SOCIAL OBLIGATION 32

Social reform and civic virtue.. 33

Conservatism and civic virtue... 38

Critical theory and social policy....................................... 41

Postmodernity and social change...................................... 44

Justice, decency and social obligation................................. 45

Conclusion... 48

3: CIVIC TRUST, CITIZENSHIP AND VOLUNTARISM...................... 50

Welfare and citizenship... 51

Postmodern society and the underclass 54

Exclusion and desert 56

Workfare and voluntarism... 58

Conclusion.. 62

4: POLITICS, VOLUNTARISM AND COMMUNITY.............................. 65

Charity, theodicy and secular values.................................... 65

Scientific charity and public morality 69

Catholicism, subsidiarity and assistencialism................................ 72

Communitarianism, emancipatory politics & cultural
defenderism 76

The new politics of postmodernity 82

Conclusion... 87

5: DECONSTRUCTING VOLUNTARISM IN A PARTNERSHIP
SOCIETY 89

Defining voluntarism and the values of the sector 91

Institutions of the sector... 97

Distinctive contribution of voluntary organisations.......................109

Conclusion...111

5

6: VOLUNTARISM, HUMAN RESOURCES AND
      PROFESSIONALISATION 113
  The role of the volunteer...113
  The scale of voluntarism 116
  Limits of voluntarism..121
  Level of professionalisation 125
  Conclusion...131
7: ROLE OF GOVERNMENT AND STATUTORY FUNDING
      OF THE VOLUNTARY SECTOR 133
  Funding and the State 139
  Dependence on private fund-raising 148
  Conclusion...154
8: EFECTIVENESS, ACCOUNTABILITY AND GOVERNANCE OF THE
      VOLUNTARY SECTOR 156
  Efficiency within the voluntary sector 156
  Public perception of standards within the voluntary sector and
      the implications of accountability 160
  Governance, management and democratisation within the voluntary
      sector 165
  Empowerment, community development and equal
      opportunities...170
  Conclusion...172
CONCLUSION 174
APPENDIX 1: METHODOLOGY OF RESEARCH 178
APPENDIX 2: QUESTIONNAIRE USED IN NATIONAL OPINION
      SURVEY...180
APPENDIX 3: QUESTIONNAIRE USED IN POSTAL SURVEY OF
      VOLUNTARY ORGANISATIONS...183
APPENDIX 4: ORGANISATIONS THAT RETURNED POSTAL
      QUESTIONNAIRE AND THAT PROVIDED REPRESENTATIVES
      TO BE INTERVIEWED 189
APPENDIX 5: OUTSTANDING DATA FOR CHAPTER 5......................193
APPENDIX 6: OUTSTANDING DATA FOR CHAPTER 6......................195
APPENDIX 7: OUTSTANDING DATA FOR CHAPTER 7......................198
BIBLIOGRAPHY 199
INDEX 208

Acknowledgements

The authors wish to acknowledge the co-operation of many voluntary and community organisations throughout Ireland that gave of their time to complete the postal questionnaire. Special thanks is given to those representatives of voluntary organisations who agreed to be interviewed. We also wish to acknowledge the generosity of so many people (far too many to mention) with their time and ideas, for which we are deeply grateful. There are three people to whom we wish to offer particular thanks: Linda Sorenson, who worked as research officer on the project; Anne Cremin who typed the manuscript with great patience and efficiency; and Paul Corcoran, who gave of his time in helping with statistical analysis of the research findings. Any errors are of course of our own making.

Introduction

This book appears at a time when civil society and voluntarism have become a core theme in Irish social policy. The publication of the Green Paper on the Community and Voluntary Sector and its Relationship with the State in 1997, as part of the National Anti-Poverty Strategy, has elevated this area of social activity to a new level of importance in public discourse. In the words of the Green Paper (Department of Social Welfare, 1997: 46), 'the voluntary sector has the potential to create a vibrant civil and active society'.

The Green Paper (1997: 6) declared its objective with clarity:

> The objective of this Green Paper is to suggest a framework for the future development of the relationship between the State and the community and voluntary sector and to facilitate a debate on the issues relevant to that relationship.

This book, which is based on two years of empirical and documentary research, is intended to be a contribution to the debate proposed by the Green Paper. The purpose of this study has been to deconstruct the meaning of civil society and the role of the voluntary sector that provides the infrastructure with reference to the social policy context. Several fundamental questions arise, which provide the chapter structure, for the book, viz.

1. Does civil society really exist or is it merely a political shibboleth?
2. What is the relationship between civic virtue and social policy?
3. What are the problems in maintaining civic trust in a divided society, and how does this phenomenon impact on the role of the voluntary sector?
4. Why do voluntary organisations exist, and how did they originate?
5. What does voluntarism mean in a partnership society?
6. How do voluntary organisations behave, and what do they do?
7. Who pays for voluntary organisations, and who benefits from them?
8. Are voluntary organisations effective, and are they democratically accountable?

Appendix 1 gives a full description of the methodology of the research. Appendixes 2–3 give an outline of the questionnaires used in a national population survey and a postal survey of 261 voluntary organisations. Appendix 4 lists the names of organisations that took part in the postal survey, as well as those that agreed to be interviewed. Appendixes 5–7 give relevant tables of data for Chapters 5, 6 and 7.

Chapter 1: Civil Society and Social Solidarity

The term 'civil society' has in recent years enjoyed something of a revival. Politicians and academics in many countries have embraced it as a prescriptive model for the future organisation of society. Exponents of civil society present it as a mediating space between the private and public spheres in a pluralist democracy. As Wedel has put it, 'a civil society exists when individuals and groups are free to form organisations that function independently and that can mediate between citizens and the State' (Wedel, 1994: 323).

Civil society is frequently equated with the voluntary or non-governmental sector. That is the focus of this book. However, there is a case for broadening this conception of civil society to embrace a wider consideration of the meaning of citizenship in contemporary society and the moral economy of the Welfare State in an era when fiscal and social conservatism has once again become dominant. These broader considerations will provide the context for the study.

In this chapter the philosophical origins of the concept of civil society will be outlined and its relevance to the present day considered in terms of political and social discourses. This will be followed by an examination of the meaning of society and individualism in the era of postmodernity. The relationship between social capital, civil society and voluntarism will then be considered. Finally, the chapter will analyse public opinion on the basis of research commissioned by UCC specially for this study. What emerges from the analysis of civil society is a concept that has, as Keane suggests, 'the capacity for making sense of such disparate phenomena as the resistance to totalitarianism, the rise of neo-conservatism, the growth of social movements and the future of the Welfare State' (Keane, 1988: 2).

Philosophical origins and political issues

In the debate about civil society the key terms—civil/civic, society, politics, community—all originate in the ancient world. For our purposes, however, the debate in the modern world is traceable to the concept of civil rights that emerged in the writings of John Locke and

11

Thomas Hobbes. The explicit use of the term is first evident in a treatise by the Scottish Enlightenment thinker, Adam Ferguson, who published *An Essay on the History of Civil Society* in 1773. In this work Ferguson explores the tensions and paradoxes inherent in the concept of civil society to the present day.

Similarly the German philosopher, Hegel, explored the concept of civil society in the definitive version of his monumental system of political and social philosophy, as it appeared in the 1821 edition of *Philosophy of Right*. For Hegel, civil society incorporates the spheres of economic relations and class formation as well as the judicial and administrative structure of the State. He does not include pre-State relations, such as the family and community, which essentially define the term 'civil society' in its most common usage today.

The debate about civil society in modern social and political thought started in the Old World, but quickly crossed the Atlantic to the New World of the American Colonies. Essential to the widening of the debate was Thomas Paine, raconteur, polemicist and commoner, who dominated progressive political thought in Britain, France and America during the age of revolutionary struggle against absolutist tyranny in the last quarter of the eighteenth century. In his highly influential pamphlet, *Common Sense*, published in 1776, Paine introduced the term 'civilised society' as a natural and potentially self-regulating form of association, counterpoised to 'Government', which was in his view, at best, a necessary and artificial evil. However, Paine was vague about what precisely he meant by civil society.

The French aristocrat Alexis De Tocqueville, who visited the United States in the 1830s, was a great deal more precise. Liberal by political persuasion, De Tocqueville is sometimes regarded as having de-politicised the term 'civil society', celebrating any form of associational activity for its own sake in the study *Democracy in America*, first published in 1835. In fact, De Tocqueville laid considerable stress on participation in local democracy as the best method for ensuring that civil association reinforced and protected democratic politics against tyranny. However, the core of his conception of civil society devolved on the health of intermediate institutions, usually the family, the community and churches. As De Tocqueville put it:

> Amongst the laws which rule human societies, there is one which seems to be more precise and clear than all others. If men are to remain civilised, or

12

to become so the art of associating together must grow and improve in the same ratio in which the equality of conditions is increased. (De Tocqueville, 1956: 202)

While De Tocqueville was commenting from the perspective of liberal individualism other contemporary thinkers addressed the concept of civil society from a very different ideological standpoint. Utopian Socialists, including Saint-Simon, Fourier and Cabet, saw the great sources of evil in society as cut-throat competition, deceit, greed and inhumanity, and the great remedy as association and co-operation to restore harmony to human life. Fourierist communities, based on the ideals of association and co-operation, were established in New Jersey, Wisconsin and Massachusetts. In Ireland Robert Owen and William Thompson advocated similar ideals. Thompson's co-operativist ideals led to the establishment of the Ralahine community in early nineteenth century Ireland (see Chapter 4).

On the other hand, Karl Marx, who along with a group of fellow German refugees in Paris during the 1830s established the League of the Just (later the Communist League) as a bulwark against capitalism, rejected civil society. Marx regarded 'civil society as an illusion that needs to be unmasked' (Hann and Dunn, 1996: 4). Later Marxists, notably Antonio Gramsci, who struggled against Fascist tyranny in twentieth century Italy, reworked the Marxist position. In his *Prison Notebook*, commenced in 1929 at the beginning of a twenty year prison sentence, Gramsci wrote:

> What we can do, for the moment, is to fix two major superstructural 'levels': the one that can be called 'civil society', and that of 'political society' or the 'State'. There two levels correspond on the one hand to the function of 'hegemony' which the dominant group exercises throughout society, and on the other hand to that of 'direct domination' or rule exercised through the State and the judicial Government. (Gramsci, 1971: 12)

For Gramsci, social inequality and class domination were exercised by a variety of cultural institutions that enabled the dominant group to impose its sense of reality on the rest of society. It was only through addressing this labyrinthine cultural complexity that the oppressed could liberate themselves and wrest control of civil society from the bourgeoisie, which had traditionally opposed popular participation. In Gramscian terms civil society was conceived as the site of alternative hegemonies.

However, as Hann and Dunn (1996: 5) observe, 'it is the liberal strand that has become almost hegemonic in most recent debates' about civil society. This is most obviously due to the transformation of Eastern Europe during the 1980s that brought about the overthrow of Stalinist tyranny. A more profound and subtle influence has been the universalisation of Western notions of freely associating individuals in a pluralistic democratic society, which have become the dominant political paradigm in postmodern society. Postmodernity represents the replacement of the standardisation, nation States and uniformity that characterised the modern era by fragmentation, globalisation and the affirmation of individual difference.

While the struggles of Eastern European dissidents, most famously the Czech playwright Vaclav Havel, highlighted the threat to civil society in State-dominated regimes, there is a growing sense of the complexity of the issues in postmodern society. Havel, now installed as the President of the Czech Republic following the Velvet Revolution, has argued for 'anti-political politics'. Recently a more sober analysis has emerged of the tide of change sweeping Eastern Europe since 1989. Hann and Dunn (1996: 8) have observed that:

> The recent revolutions in Eastern Europe were the first in human history *not* to be concerned with establishing some form of rational Utopia. These societies (post-communist) are seen as characterised by unfettered egoism and consumerism. Only individuals exist, and they are allegedly devoid of significant human relationships.

Hann and Dunn conclude that 'civil society is no longer, in the mid 1990s, the emotive slogan that it became for many East European intellectuals in the 1980s' (1996: 9). They cite the iconic figure of Vaclav Havel in support of their case. Havel (1993) has admitted to the existence of 'a post-communist nightmare'. The Hungarian-born philanthropist, George Soros, who financed the movement towards civil society in Eastern Europe during the 1980s, has also been critical of post-communist society (*The Guardian*, 18 January, 1997).

Similarly, Anderson (1996: 99), writing about the 'mythical archetype' of Siberia, challenges the view 'in both popular thought and in social theory for the *complete absence* of any kind of autonomously managed or meaningful public space' in Soviet society. He asserts:

> Unlike the coffee houses or political parties in Euro-American society, civil society in Siberia was harboured within different 'citizenship regimes',

14

which formed restricted yet significant channels for economic and political practice. The past tense is deliberate: the assault on forms of civic entitlement and participation has never been greater than within the current politics of privatisation. (Anderson, 1996: 100)

The equation of civil society with a generic Euro-American State is clearly an ideological position that has more to do with post-Cold War politics than serious social analysis. There are, manifestly, various definitions of civil society in the history of social and political thought, as outlined above. But the core distinction is probably a lexical conflict of meanings inherent in the term 'civil society', between 'citizen society' and 'market society'. This ambiguity is apparent in the German term for civil society, *burgerliche Gesellschaft*, translatable as both 'citizen society' and 'bourgeoisie society'.

Cohen and Arato (1992) have demonstrated how these two counterpoised meanings might be harmoniously reconciled without either becoming dominant over the other. They advocate a three-part model of social structure differentiating between (1) the activities of commerce, (2) the administrative powers of the State and (3) civil society that fosters a vibrant lifeworld of symbols and solidarities. Cohen and Arato (1992: ix) consequently define civil society as 'a sphere of social interaction between economy and State, composed above all of the intimate sphere (especially the family), the sphere of associations (especially voluntary associations), social movements, and forms of public communications . . . institutionalised and generalised through laws'.

Cohen and Arato are deeply indebted to the German sociologist Jurgen Habermas, whose ideas inform their analysis. Habermas has directly linked communication and solidarity: 'communicative action is a switching station for the energies of social solidarity'. (Habermas, 1987: 57) Even more fundamentally, they adopt Habermas' distinction between the lifeworld as a world of symbols and solidarities and the system defined by the instrumental relations of politics and commerce. This influence is most evident in their delimitation of the institutions of civil society: 'institutions that must be co-ordinated communicately appear under the heading of civil society' (Cohen and Arato, 1992: 480). In this assertion, Cohen and Arato firmly place civil society in the lifeworld, and in identifying communication as the distinctive feature of civil society they draw upon the constitutional features of the lifeworld that

15

distinguish it from the political and economic sub-systems. It is, as Cohen and Arato put it, a *posttraditional* view designed to meet postmodern conditions.

The definition offered by Cohen and Arato creatively avoids conceptual ambiguity. But deeper, longer term historical issues are also at stake. While much of the current social condition is novel, there is clearly an on-going debate about the nature of society and the role of the individual. The debate about civil society is emblematic of this more fundamental debate in an age when the grand historical narrative (Christianity, Marxism, etc.) has lost its persuasive force, at least in Western society. The replacement of the modern project of the nation State, latterly the Welfare State, by 'postmodernity' raises larger questions about the idea of 'the social' to which we must now turn.

Postmodernity, society and individualism

We live in a society defined by risk, polarisation, global markets, chronic change and fragmentation. As Stokes and Knight (1997) have observed, 'today we seem to be plunging into a chaotic, privatised future, recapturing medieval extremes of wealth and squalor' (*The Independent*, 15 January 1997).

On the face of it, our civilisation is both atomised and fractured. Yet there is a paradox that confounds such conclusions. While the self, in the form of the independent citizen, may have become sovereign in the choice of lifestyles, solidarity is maintained by recognition-based social relations such as love, friendship, trust, empathy and compassion, charity, altruism and mutualism and the willingness to make sacrifices for others. In short, as Berking observes, 'these are cognitive, normative and emotional competencies which anything but reduce interest in the other to the mode of a merely strategic interaction' (Berking, 1996: 192). Love and friendship clearly belong to the private sphere. Charity, altruism and mutualism exist in the space between Government and market called 'the voluntary or third sector'. These virtues point towards the existence of active citizenship in the form of participation and dutiful citizenship in the form of obligation towards others. Trust, empathy and compassion are the common elements that transcend utilitarian individualism and define solidary individualism. This is the essential contradiction of contemporary Western society that provides the basis for civic trust in an increasingly fragmented and polarised social order.

Berking has observed that 'the triumphant advance of utilitarian values, which now seem to oblige the individual to secure and augment his own advantage, is today described under the heading detraditionalisation and individualisation, above all the cumulative effect of the process of cultural modernisation' (Berking, 1996: 191). The assumption that the modern individual is less committed to the other than his/her traditional counterpart is doubtful. Carmen argues that the reverse is the case:

> Traditional society is essentially non-participant. It deploys people by kinship into communities isolated by each other and from the centre. Modernity, on the other hand, is essentially a mode of communication and participation. What makes communication possible, the sociological pivot upon which hinges the activation of psychic mobility, is the acquisition of literacy. An increase in literacy and therefore an increase in the capacity to empathise is the very yeast, which permeates the system of self-sustaining growth and mass consumption. This is the *ne plus ultra* of modernity and by implication of development . . . Empathy is the bridge, which makes transition from traditional to modern ways feasible (Carmen, 1990: 4).

Other commentators who have sought to examine the nature and quality of trust and its connection with co-operation and prosperity have also discovered a positive correlation between modernity and civil society (Fukuyama, 1995; Putnam, 1993). Fukuyuma found that developed societies such as the USA, Germany and Japan were high-trust societies compared with less developed societies such as Latin Catholic countries and China, which he concluded were low-trust societies. Similarly, in Italy Putnam found higher levels of civic trust in the more developed Northern region, 'Padania', than in the less developed South. We must therefore conclude that, despite its tendencies towards fragmentation and polarisation, postmodernity has engendered social participation and more sophisticated forms of communication between people that promote empathy and trust. This is the paradox of contemporary civilisation.

On the face of it, this is a two-world theory of an economic world defined by utilitarian values and a social world defined by solidaristic values. However, Fukuyuma (1995) and Putnam (1993) contend in their theses on trust and solidaristic values in the social sphere that these are positively correlated with the creation of prosperity in the economic sphere. In reality they claim to have discovered a civilisational configuration between altruism and self-interest. However, it should be noted that the three fastest growing post-War economies were Japan, France and Italy—one high-trust and two low-trust societies by Fukuyama's reckoning. A more realistic assessment of their position is that it represents a reconfiguration of 'the social' in an era when neo-conservatism and global capital have become dominant and 'the social' increasingly privatised.

For neo-conservatives there is no civil society, only individual enterprise and self-reliance. Hayek has contended that 'the social' is merely 'something which has developed as a practice of individual action in the course of social evolution' (Hayek, 1976: 78). For Hayek, 'the social' was an abhorrent concept that conjured up images of totalitarianism. In his book *The Mirage of Social Justice* (1976) he equates the pursuit of equality with tyranny. Conservative social theorists have challenged the normative basis of social solidarity, which they view as creating a dependent underclass (Gilder, 1981; Murray, 1984; Marsland, 1995, 1996). Marsland (1995: 4) has likened welfare to a 'cancer in the body politic' and added that 'it has also spread its contagion through more and more organs of society'. He concluded that 'only markets can provide effectively for the range and ambition of human wants and needs' (Marsland, 1996: 140).

Neo-conservative politicians have taken the debate into the public arena. They have attacked social solidarity as the embodiment of collectivism. In their zealous efforts to destroy collectivism, they have sought to deny the existence of 'the social'. In Margaret Thatcher's famous aphorism, 'there is no such thing as society', (*The Sunday Times*, 9 November, 1988). Thatcher went on to elaborate her ideas in a controversial speech to the Assembly of the Church of Scotland, in which she asserted that it was, above all, within the family that the 'the nursery of civic virtue' lay. She contended that the family should be the basis on which Governments ought to construct their policies for 'welfare, education and care' (Thatcher, quoted in Squires, 1990: 5). Neo-conservatism has, therefore, sought to write the obituary of 'the social' and looked backwards nostalgically to Tocquevilleian visions of smaller units of social responsibility, notably the family and the community. The denial of 'the social' is, consequently, not a denial of social responsibility. It simply means that the social rights of the entitled citizen of the Welfare State are replaced by the social obligations of the dutiful citizen in a reconstituted order where the market replaces society as the arbiter of moral values.

Teeple (1995: 150–151) has characterised the much-vaunted triumph of neo-conservatism and the global market as the coming tyranny, observing that:

> Capitalism must increasingly confront the world that it has made, the results of its own expansion: seriously degraded nature, an increasingly impoverished working class, growing political autocracy and declining legitimacy, and new forms of resistance . . . Here, largely unfettered by political considerations, is a tyranny unfolding—an economic regime of unaccountable rules, a totalitarianism not of the political but of the economic.

Other commentators have taken a more optimistic view detecting a new complexity in which a more democratic citizenship can emerge. Walzer (1983) has suggested a break with the old normative idealism embodied in collectivist and universal notions of 'the social' and advocated new thinking around pluralist frameworks of complex equality that involves taking democratic rights beyond traditional conceptions of citizenship.

Behind Walzer's vision is the assumption that culture and society shape the nature of Government. This is true to a degree. It is essential to the Tocquevillian vision of the pivotal role of intermediate institutions as the generative force in society. However, an older tradition of thought, stretching from Aristotle to Montesquieu, suggests that fundamentally the State shapes society, not the other way round. If we accept this view we are thinking not about civil society in the all-embracing sense envisaged by de Tocqueville, but about the Roman virtue of *civitas*, i.e. public-spiritedness, sacrifice for the community and, of course, active citizenship.

Welfare, civil society and voluntary action

At the core of the contemporary debate about civil society is the relationship between welfare and citizenship. Much of this debate has devolved on a crude distinction between individualism and collectivism. The moral and emotional meanings attached to both terms have obscured as much as they have enlightened. Inherent in the debate about these social forms lies a deeper distinction about alternative conceptions of the self, the good life and human potential and purpose. As Marquand puts it:

> On the one side of the divide are those who view the self as a static

19

bundle of preferences and the good life as one in which individuals pursue their own preferences without interference from others. On the other are those for whom the self is a governing and developing moral entity and the good life one in which individuals learn to adopt higher preferences in place of lower ones. On one side of the divide stress is laid on satisfaction; on the other on effort, engagement and activity (*The Guardian*, 28 October 1996).

In this prescient comment, Marquand essentially differentiates between the independent citizen and the active citizen. The active citizen forms the cornerstone of civil society, since s/he has embraced a form of solidary individualism that addresses the imperative of the common good.

The relative influences of individualism and collectivism have waxed and waned throughout the short history of the post-War Welfare State. The founders of the Welfare State enthusiastically embraced the concept of the entitled citizen, whose rights to healthcare, housing, education and a guaranteed income went hand-in-hand with a rigorous Fabian ethic of duty. In their view the entitled citizen must also be an active citizen engaged with the community, since the redistribution of wealth, on which the Welfare State edifice rested, had created a just and therefore moral social order, in which the citizen could live an active and fulfilling life (see Chapter 2).

By the mid-1970s a moral vacuum had opened between the rhetoric and the reality of the Welfare State. Into this vacuum stepped the anti-collectivists denouncing the Welfare State for creating a dependency culture and sapping the moral fibre of society. Marquand has suggested that the Welfare State had created a hedonistic society, in which collective action and collective provision had become sources of 'moral escapism, encouraging those who took part in them to shelter from the consequences of their own actions, and so engendering a corrosive culture of guilt' (*The Guardian*, 28 October 1996).

But this moralistic individualism, based on the Victorian virtues of self-reliance and enterprise, proved to be as fragile and even more ephemeral in its influence. A moral order founded on the market is a contradiction in terms, since the market is by definition amoral, antinomian and subversive of all values—except the value of free exchange. The moral individualism of Thatcherism and Reaganomics quickly mutated into hedonistic individualism. The rhetoric of self-reliance and patriotic sacrifice stood in stark contrast to the selfish vices

20

of wealth accumulation and its accompanying lifestyle of self-gratification at all costs.

Not surprisingly, as we entered the 1990s a new debate began about the values of civic trust. In this debate the good society has been recast as civil society. This development essentially represents a swing back towards collectivism, since it promotes a new form of communitarianism (Etzioni, 1994; Fukuyama, 1995). However, to describe this trend as a reassertion of the collectivist values of the Welfare State would be simplistic. What the 'new communitarianism' of the exponents of civil society seeks to do is to reconcile the globalised market with a form of active citizenship in which the individual seeks to achieve a moral commitment through involvement in the community. In a sense this is a cross-cutting definition that defies the distinction between individualism and collectivism. That is both its strength and its weakness.

The exponents of civil society in the contemporary debate about the moral economy of welfare view reciprocal responsibility and social wellbeing as the basis of 'social capital'. Fukuyuma (1995: 26) asserts that:

> Social capital is a capability that arises from the prevalence of trust in a society or certain parts of it. It can be embodied in the smallest and most basic social group, the family as well as the largest of all groups the nation, and in all other groups in between. Social capital differs from all other forms of human capital insofar as it is usually transmitted through cultural mechanisms like religion, tradition or historical habit.

Social capital therefore, comprises the institutional relationships of a vibrant civil society, based on solidary individualism and active citizenship, from extended families to neighbourhood networks, community groups to religious organisations, youth clubs to parent-teacher associations, local businesses to local public services, playgroups to the police on the beat (Borrie Report, 1994: 307-8). At the heart of civil society is empathy, compassion, trust and participation. This is the basis of the 'good society' that we all yearn to belong to in the midst of uncertainty, scepticism, disillusion and institutional fragmentation. Consequently, the pluralisation of lifestyles and the search for meaning in the midst of uncertainty has stimulated a revitalisation of the concept of civil society as a means for resolving the problems of contemporary society.

The renewal of civil society has been associated with demands for a larger role for voluntary welfare provision in both western society and the former Soviet Bloc. The voluntary sector is perceived as (1) an alternative to State bureaucracy and professional elitism and (2) a public space between Government and market. Civil society in its reinvigorated form is presented by its advocates as a democratic movement based on the concept of active citizenship as opposed to the dependent status imposed by the entitled citizenship of the Welfare State. The emphasis of active citizenship is on participation in the decision-making process leading to empowerment of the citizen (Etzioni, 1994).

According to the concept of civil society, communities, neighbourhoods, voluntary associations and churches are the basic building blocks of society because they teach civic virtues such as trust and co-operation (Etzioni, 1994; Fukuyuma, 1995; Keane, 1988; Putnam, 1993). These 'new communitarians' promote the fostering of intermediate institutions, i.e. families, neighbourhoods and schools, in civil society. They view these intermediate institutions as the source of moral and social cohesion in the globalised market society. At the same time they regard a revitalised civil society as a bulwark against an overweening Welfare State that, in their view, has lost its legitimacy because of its remote bureaucratic structure and domination by professional elites. As Landry and Mulgan (1995: 6) put it:

> Associational life in the form of family networks, networks of interest groups and others have often provided an important glue through which the individual and the group have been bound together in some larger whole. Traditionally this 'civic' realm has provided the means for people to transcend pure individual self interest in the name of the public good. More recently, as the State has lost its legitimacy as the upholder and arbiter of that public interest, other types of civic association have come to seem more important.

Salamon (1994) suggests that 'a virtual associational revolution' is taking place throughout the world, creating a global voluntary sector. It is defined by several core characteristics:
- structured organisations
- located outside the format apparatus of the State
- not intended to distribute profits from activities to a set of shareholders or directors
- self-governing
- involving significant private, voluntary effort (Salamon, 1994: 5).

The impetus for the global associational revolution has come both from the bottom-up and from the top-down. Eastern Europe provides the most dramatic example, with organisations such as Solidarity in Poland and the Civic Forum Movement in Czechoslovakia capturing the imagination of the world. Less well reported were the environmentalist movements in Eastern Europe during the Communist era: the Danube Circle, which opposed the siting of a hydroelectric plant on the Danube in Hungary, and Arche, the environmental organisation that campaigned against acid rain in East Germany by tying thousands of bed sheets to apartment roofs and then recording the pollution accumulated. These activists in Eastern Europe (including the Soviet Union) described 'their efforts as the creating of a 'civil society', a society in which individuals have the right not only to speak out as individuals, but also to join together in organisations' (Salamon, 1994: 5).

This pressure for bottom-up change through voluntary organisation was perhaps most dramatic in Eastern Europe because it brought down the communist form of Government and its hegemonic system of control. However, the 'virtual associational revolution' was by definition a global movement touching most continents. The so-called urban popular movement in Mexico and elsewhere in Latin America is characteristic of grass roots political activities against Government oppression in the Americas. In Africa a 'new wind' of change has given rise to grass roots political and environmental organisations, notably in Nigeria, usually of a non-profit voluntary nature. Chopko, the Indian environmentalist movement, arose from a spontaneous effort by rural residents to protect a endangered forest by literally linking their arms around it.

Support in the West for the expansion of voluntary organisations was distinctive because of its top-down character and its association with the scaling down of the Welfare State. Neo-conservatives were at the forefront of this process, notably Margaret Thatcher in Britain and Ronald Reagan in the United States. Reagan opposed 'Big Government' *per se*. Thatcher took a more radical line by calling for the dismantling not only of the Welfare State, 'but also the organised voluntary sector and leave social care wholly to volunteers' (quoted in Salamon, 1994: 8). She described volunteers as 'the heart of all our social welfare provision' (quoted in Salamon, 1994: 8). Support for voluntarism has not been unique to neo-conservative Governments. The Socialist President of France, François Mitterand, sought to liberalise taxes on 'social economy organisations' during the 1980s. However, social economy organisations in France (like Germany) are 70% supported by public funding, creating a symbiotic relationship between the State and the voluntary/community sector.

The Irish Government has been strongly supportive of voluntary organisations through the National Social Services Board, originally established in 1971. The publication of a Green Paper on the Voluntary and Community Sector and its Relationship with the State by the Irish Government in 1997 firmly locates Ireland within the European social market model that favours partnership.

Critics of civil society point out that the real emphasis is on the dutiful citizen engaged in self-help. In the context of the atomised individualism and fragmented social order we live in, there is an element of unreality about the larger claims made for the concept of civil society as an alternative to State welfare. As Kramer (1981: 283) puts it:

> Voluntarism is no substitute for services that can best be delivered by Government, particularly if coverage, equity and entitlements are valued . . . there is a danger that those who have jumped on the bandwagon of the era of limits, signalling the end of the Welfare State by advocating more voluntarism, are being co-opted by others who share less concern with social justice than with tax reduction.

Clearly, it is quite unsustainable to suggest that the needs of the most disadvantaged can be met by the voluntary sector. Civil society based purely on the principle of private altruism would not be a civilised society. Indeed, there is no essential link between civil society and civilised society—contrary to Paine's view. Civil society has had a chequered political history. The Nazi party undermined the Weimar Republic in Germany by infiltrating local organisations. It should not be forgotten that the Mafia is an intermediate institution.

Closer to home, paramilitary organisations in Northern Ireland have exerted considerable influence in their communities by establishing a significant presence within some voluntary organisations. At a more general level some small local groups in Ireland have been thoroughly illiberal in their responses to drug abusers and HIV victims. Pseudo-religious cults, with their internal cultures of intimidation, psychological domination of the individual and sometimes violent agendas, further highlight the dark side of associational life. In a climate of increasing ethnic conflict, manifested in Ireland by communal hostility towards the

24

Travelling community and political refugees, intermediate institutions can be anything but civil.

It is the core contention of this study that civil society that is genuinely civilised is meaningless outside a Welfare State ethos in contemporary western civilisation. To argue that Rotary Clubs, Red Cross Chapters and local community groups can provide social protection in the era of globalised capital would not be a tenable position. However, civil society connected to generative political strategies, based on more complex ideas of equality and a more empowering concept of citizenship, is a vibrant and powerful concept of civic renewal in an era of social fragmentation. Irish public opinion strongly supports this vision of civil society (see below) as integral to a Welfare State ethos, in which voluntary action prospers in a mixed economy of welfare in partnership (rather than competition) with the State and social citizenship. The EU Comité des Sages (1996: 14), which addressed the future of civic and social rights in Europe, shares this vision, stating that while in a global economy competitiveness is a 'fixed imperative', it 'cannot be improved by dismantling the Welfare State'. Instead it called for developing social rights and 'rejuvenating social dialogue'.

Pluralism is at the core of this vision. The Report of the Commission on the Future of the Voluntary Sector (1996: 22) in the UK observed in this regard that 'the pluralism that is a characteristic of a healthy civil society implies a diversity of ideas, institutions and interests that sometimes appears chaotic'. This 'creative chaos', as the distinguished German sociologist Professor Ralf Dahrendorf has put it, goes to the heart of the democratic contribution that the voluntary sector makes to the dynamic of civil society. The esteemed British social policy scholar, Professor David Donnisson told the Commission on the Future of the Voluntary Sector (1996: 22) that:

> what could become damaging tyrannies and *abuses* should be kept in check, partly by strong democratic civic leadership, which establishes and polices the limits of tolerable behaviour and ensures that groups that might be neglected gain a hearing and partly by competition between agencies expressing different interests and views. If this system includes a sufficiently rich and well informed mixture of agencies capable of working in these ways and power holders in the public and private sectors are capable to responding to them, it will help to make the society which it operates more democratic.

The Commission (1996: 15) itself concluded in this regard that 'the relationship between voluntary bodies and democratic institutions can be seen in different ways—either as a contribution in their own right to the vitality of civil society or as a check on abuses of power'.

The EU Comité des Sages (1996: 53) went a great deal further; asserting that:

> democratic consultation must give due weight to the traditional social partners but cannot be restricted to them alone. It must also encompass new players, and in particular non-Governmental organisations.

What is clear is that the voluntary sector is characterised by a dynamic diversity that contributes to the well-being of civil society, outside the confines of the market and the State. Citizens contribute to the voluntary sector both as individuals and collectively, informally and formally through organisations and without payment or as salaried staff. Voluntary organisations exist at national level and at local community level, in myriad forms both large and small. Some are traditional and paternalistic. Others are transparently democratic, controlled and operated by users. Many voluntary organisations have close partnership relationships with the State, often depending on statutory funding for survival. Yet others challenge the State through vigorous social movements (e.g. environmental, peace, gay and lesbian, feminist, anti-racist, etc.) that some see as 'a people's opposition'. In this diversity lies the strength and weakness of the voluntary sector and, indeed, the limitations of civil society. The future is in this diversity but not as an alternative to the Welfare State. The mainstream of the voluntary sector in the social market economy is clearly shaped by its symbiotic relationship with the State. Only in liberal market economies such as the USA, where the State contributes 10% of funding, are things different.

Public opinion, social engagement and active citizenship

Peillon has conclusively demonstrated 'striking popular support' for the Welfare State in Ireland (Peillon, 1995: 3). The International Social Survey programme repeated in 1990 a 1985 survey of attitudes towards the role of Government. Ten countries were included. Northern Ireland was categorised as a separate geo-political entity to Britain. Other countries included were Australia, USA, Hungary, Italy, Norway, Israel and Germany (East and West). Only former East Germany scored a higher aggregate index of support for the Welfare State than Ireland. It was also notable that Northern Ireland was closer to Ireland in its support for the Welfare State than to Britain, with which it shares a common welfare system (Peillon, 1995: 3–21).

A national opinion survey, commissioned by UCC for this study, has also indicated a high level of support for the Welfare State. This survey found that 42% of respondents were in favour of increased taxes being used to improve welfare services provided directly by the State rather than the State passing money to voluntary organisations for them to provide the welfare services. 31% of respondents disagreed with this proposition and 27% were unable to answer the question. Stronger support for statutory services among the volunteer section of the population was evident in another part of the UCC research into the voluntary sector. A second survey of 223 voluntary organisations, carried out by UCC, found that 54% of respondents were in favour of the State providing more of the services their organisation provided. Only 9% of organisations were in favour of the State having less involvement, and the remaining 37% of organisations were in favour of a continuation of the present level of State involvement. The majority of voluntary organisations (54%) were also opposed to the proposition that there is an over-reliance on the Welfare State among the Irish population (see Chapters 5 and 6 for further details on the research).

A variety of factors may explain the high level of support for the Welfare State in Ireland. It may be due to Ireland's late development as an urban industrial country. The commonality of popular support for the Welfare State with Northern Ireland suggests that particular cultural factors may be important. The shared memory of the Famine, emigration and endemic poverty makes Ireland unique in the developed world. Peillon suggests that this high level of support for the Welfare State in Ireland 'may also be linked with the widespread (but by no means universal) character of many social services' (Peillon, 1995: 19). Probably the most important factor in explaining support for the Welfare State in Ireland is the high level of consensus that currently exists within Irish society, epitomised by Partnership 2000.

The sense of national commitment to the Welfare State has not displaced a vibrant voluntary sector; rather a powerful commitment to partnership defines this relationship. The national opinion survey, commissioned by UCC, found that 32% of the population had given their services without pay to a voluntary organisation. This finding concurs with the results of research on the extent of volunteering in the general population in Ireland, carried out by the Dublin-based Policy Research Centre, published in 1993, which found that 39% of those interviewed had been involved in at least one voluntary activity within the month prior to interview (Ruddle and O'Connor, 1993: 57). There are variations in the extent of participation between different groups in the population.

The UCC-commissioned national opinion survey has found that 43% of the middle class members of the population (ABC1) had volunteered their services to a voluntary organisation, in contrast to 25% of working class members of the population (C2DE) and 34% of farmers. The results also provide evidence of a substantial under-representation of the 15–34 age group, who constitute 42% of the total population and of whom only 27% have given their services to a voluntary organisation. This result can be contrasted with the 35–54 age group, who make up 33% of the population and of whom 42% have given their services to a voluntary organisation. There was no major gender difference in the levels of participation—31% of men and 33% of women had given their services to a voluntary organisation (these findings will be discussed in detail in Chapter 6; see Appendix 1 for a full description of the methodology of the research).

Comparative European research seems to indicate that similar patterns are evident across several countries. After reviewing the research findings on the extent of volunteering in Belgium, Bulgaria, Denmark, France, Germany, Great Britain, Ireland, Netherlands, Slovakia and Sweden, Gaskin and Smith (1995: 63) have concluded that:

> Volunteering in Europe cuts across all social groupings and includes people with all kinds of personal characteristics. There is a tendency for the rate of volunteering to be related to social class; more volunteers are employed and of relatively high status, in terms of education, occupation, social grade and income. While this has been accepted in individual countries like Great Britain; the evidence from this study is that it is a widespread tendency, but not universal.

The Report of the Commission on the Future of the Voluntary Sector (1996) in the UK, referring to the situation in England and Wales, has drawn attention to the fact that many organisations have experienced a decline in the numbers of their volunteers over the past decade, particularly the more traditional welfare agencies which have tended to rely on a certain type of volunteer. The reasons for this decline in the attraction of volunteers to traditional service provision voluntary organisations are cited as:

> Changing patterns of work with the entry of more women into the paid labour market, has severely reduced the pool of 'traditional' volunteers in some sectors, a situation exacerbated by the increasing caring responsibilities taken on by many women; while the rapid growth of new groups and charities more in tune with the attitudes and values of people today have further sapped support from more traditional agencies. (Report of the Commission on the Future of the Voluntary Sector, 1996: 75)

Knight and Stokes (1996: 8) have argued that the decline in the extent of volunteering among established voluntary organisations is part of a trend of decreasing participation in the traditional pillars of civil society in the UK, e.g. trade unions, mutual aid associations, the churches, political parties and social networks. On the other hand, there is very strong evidence of increased membership of environmental organisations (Knight and Stokes, 1996: 12). Demonstrably voluntary activity shifts with changing social trends. In the Irish context, the UCC survey of voluntary organisations found that 39% of respondents had found it more difficult than it was in the past to recruit volunteers. More traditional service provision-orientated organisations were the most affected by these difficulties. The apparent emergence of the problem of civic disengagement among the general population has also been greatly influenced by what Kramer calls 'the growing interdependency of the Government and the voluntary sector, which has resulted in a pervasive and complex mingling of public and private funds and functions, producing quangos and para-Governmental organisations' (Kramer, 1990: 3). Kramer goes on to ask whether increased bureaucratisation and professionalisation associated with the delivery of established public services will result in the crowding out of small, local and minority organisations by the large national agencies (Kramer, 1990: 6).

None the less, Knight and Stokes' contention that the decline in active volunteer participation in traditional service provision organisations represents an undermining of civil society must be viewed with caution, in the light of the adoption by many organisations of the principles of user empowerment and community development. The UCC survey of voluntary organisations has found that together with 51% of respondents who felt that the issue of empowerment had become more important, 53% of organisations felt that the community aspect of their work had become far more relevant since their foundation.

Evidence of a commitment to a civil society, based on solidary individualism and social citizenship, would also seem to be apparent from further findings of the UCC survey. The survey found that 76% of the population who have had involvement with voluntary organisations disagreed with the proposition that 'to succeed in this life, you must grab what you can and not worry about other members of society too much'. Only 61% of the population who had no involvement with voluntary organisations disagreed with the proposition. A commitment to active citizenship and civic engagement based on a vibrant voluntary sector would seem to be a key ingredient of civil society. The remaining questions are (1) whether solidary individualism can be extended to all sections of society, based on the development of 'social capital' and (2) how entitlements can be assured if communitarianism is an uphill struggle in an age of polarisation, risk and fragmentation.

Conclusion

This chapter has argued that modern society is increasingly characterised by detraditionalisation and individualisation. However, postmodern society, despite its tendencies towards fragmentation and polarisation, has also engendered empathy and trust between people. The two faces of the social order are characterised by a set of utilitarian values, such as self-help, embraced by neo-conservatives, and on the other side a commitment to altruism and mutualism, which is the core of civic virtue. The exponents of civil society view reciprocal responsibility and mutualism as the basis of civic virtue. A reinvigorated civil society is promoted as an appropriate response to contemporary social problems. It is also been argued that at the core of a revitalised civil society are intermediate institutions such as family networks, interest groups and voluntary organisations.

Critics of civil society argue that voluntarism is no substitute for services best delivered by the State. Research by the UCC has confirmed previous studies that extensive support exists for the Welfare State in Ireland. It has also demonstrated that Ireland, in common with several other European countries, has a vibrant voluntary sector which, however, faces difficulties in relation to recruitment, particularly among more traditional service provision organisations. It can be argued that difficulties in the recruitment of volunteers and evidence of civic disengagement represent a decline in civil society. However, there is also evidence that many voluntary organisations are increasingly adopting the philosophies of community development and empowerment and mutating into democratically based bottom-up communitarian organisations. The UCC research has also provided evidence that attitudes supportive of civil society are widely held among the Irish population, particularly among the section of the population which has had involvement with voluntary organisations. This is probably due to the high level of consensus about the need for partnership. However, concern remains about civic disengagement and the meaning of civic virtue in an increasingly polarised and fragmented society, where universalised values of citizenship and social rights are under threat. That is the subject of the next two chapters.

Chapter Two: Civic Virtue, Rights and Social Obligation

The purpose of this chapter is to examine the ideals that have shaped social policy. It juxtaposes the Fabian concept of civic virtue, based on universalist ideals of citizenship and human rights, with more recent perspectives emerging from neo-conservatism and critical theory. Universalist and collectivist values are contrasted with the postmodern emphasis on the individual as an autonomous moral agent and the growth of particularism arising from contemporary social movements and identity politics that advocates different rather than shared social values. Finally, the chapter looks at a concept of social obligation, based on shared vulnerabilities, as the basis for civic virtue in a just and decent society.

Both civil society and civic virtue are concerned with defining the relationship between the individual and the social and are firmly rooted in the intellectual traditions of Western civilisation. They are visible in the doctrines of natural law and the political philosophies of classical Greece and republican Rome.

The Greek word *arete* is translated as 'virtue' and means the quality which entitles any institution or individual to be called good. Plato divided human virtue into four elements: wisdom, courage, temperance and justice. For Plato, justice is simultaneously a part of human virtue and the bond that joins people together in society. It is virtue that makes an individual both good and social. This construct is the first and fundamental principle of Plato's political philosophy. The Renaissance Italian philosopher, Machiavelli, reflecting on the practical lessons to be learnt from the fall of the Roman Republic, cites civic virtue in a people as the essential ingredient for a free society. He equates virtue with vigour in both the human body and the body politic, and concludes that where civic virtue is lacking the people are corrupt and tyranny is inevitable. For Machiavelli, the two great forces that govern society are fortune and virtue. Fortune is a capricious power, incalculable and often irresistible, influencing human destiny from without. But people are not simply the victims of fortune, they can seek to control their own destinies. The power that enables them to do so is civic virtue, and the more virtuous a people, the freer is a society.

Civic humanists of the Renaissance period maintained that civic virtue was essential to the maintenance of 'the civil life'. As Thomas Starkey (1533: 27), put it in his *Dialogue*, 'the civil life consists of living together in good and politic order, being ever ready to do good to another, and as it were conspiring together in all virtue and honesty'. That is the moral in the tale of civic virtue, that is as true today as it was in earlier historical epochs.

The breakdown of the traditional feudal order and the collapse of the universal Catholic Church necessitated a new basis for the organisation of society. However, secular and Christian traditions share core values. They are both concerned with the creation of a 'moral community' as the foundation for social life. In each tradition the concept of 'virtue' is perceived as fundamental to the existence of a moral community. Furthermore, both advocate the universalisation of these ideals. Fabianism has epitomised the presumption of civic virtue and the creation of a civil society in the era of modernity, as the basis of a just and stable social order (Seligman, 1996: 201–2).

Social reform and civic virtue

The Fabian tradition, which has dominated social policy discourse from the beginning, represents the modernist exposition of the ideals of civic virtue. Fabianism, which began in 1883, had a number of distinctive qualities that have shaped the discipline of social policy at a fundamental level. First, it was the product of the English and Irish socially-minded intellectuals, notably Sidney and Beatrice Webb, H. G. Wells, and George Bernard Shaw. Shaw, who was the founder of the Fabian Society, defined its objectives as 'the collection and publication of authentic and impartial statistical tracts' in order to make 'the public conscious of the evil condition of society under the present system' (Shaw, 1896: 7). The Fabians rejected the dominant influence of Marxist socialism in Europe. They drew their social idealism from the American economist Henry George and advocates of a more just society based on equality. George's gospel, which was outlined in his classic work, *Poverty and Progress*, first published in 1879, found a sympathetic audience on this side of the Atlantic. He argued that the remedy to poverty lay in a Single Tax levied on the value of land exclusive of improvements, and the abolition of all taxes on industry and thrift. During a period when agrarian agitation in Ireland was a major political issue, coupled with the presence of severe distress among crofters in Scotland and a deep agricultural depression throughout the United Kingdom, 'George's remedy, the Single Tax, was not so drastic as land rationalisation' (Pelling, 1965: 18).

In Ireland the ideal of land reform and social equality had been championed by James Fintan Lalor as early as the 1840s. Michael Davitt, who met Henry George and was impressed by his schemes, made tenurial rights the basis of the Land League founded in 1878. His book *The Fall of Feudalism in Ireland,* published in 1904, was influenced by similar struggles in Russia, where land redistribution had become the cornerstone of social reform. The emphasis on land redistribution in Ireland and Russia reflected the pre-industrial state of the economies in both societies.

The influence of the mutualistic ideal of social obligation on Fabianism is usually associated with the Scottish scholar, Thomas Davidson, who spent a considerable part of his life in the United States. While both Owenite and Ruskinite utopianism were clearly also present in Davidson's mutualism, he in fact attributed his views to an unorthodox Catholic thinker, Antonio Rosmini-Serbati, who had founded the Brethren of Charity. In harmony with Rosminian thought, Davidson had advocated a reformation of mankind replacing individualism by the civic virtues of co-operation and brotherhood. The centrality of the ideal of social obligation to the Fabian movement has been clearly delineated by Beatrice Webb as a core influence guiding her work in the English Poor Law Commission (1905-9). She declared:

> The whole theory of the mutual obligation between the individual and the State, which I find myself working out in my poor law scheme, is taken straight out of the nobler aspect of the medieval manor. It will come as a new idea to the present generation— it is really a very old one that has been thrust out of sight in order to attain some measure of equality of political rights. There are some who wish to attain a socialist State by the assertion of economic equality—they desire to force the property-owners to yield to the non-property owners. I prefer to have the forward movement based on the obligation of each individual to serve. (*Our Partnership,* 1948: 385)

The preoccupation of the founders of Fabianism with the concept of social obligation became the guiding philosophical inspiration of the reformist tradition in social policy. Titmuss, in his classic study *The Gift*

Relationship (1970), lays down the philosophical roots of the discipline. This study, which takes the blood transfusion service as a microcosm of the British Welfare State, devolves on the key role of altruism in society. Titmusss argues that 'the ways in which society organises and structures its social institutions—particularly its health and welfare systems— can encourage or discourage the altruistic in man' (Titmuss, 1970: 225).

The Fabians were, however, far from being utopians nostalgically yearning for earlier and simpler forms of social organisation. They shared the utilitarianism which had guided social policy in Britain and Ireland since the poor law debates of the 1820s and 1830s. But their utilitarianism differed from the harsh rationalism of Bentham. It was tempered by the philosophical radicalism of John Stuart Mill and their belief in a more mutualistic social order advocated by the Irish economist William Thompson. As Cole and Postgate (1961: 423) have put it, 'Fabianism was the new Benthamism, seeking 'the greatest happiness of the greatest number', not by means of *laissez-faire*, but through the collective control of the economic forces of society, and regarding Socialism as simply the logical consummation of a progressive policy of social reform'.

This view to an extent trivialises the utilitarianism of the Fabians since it ignores the moral sense inherent in their philosophy that sought to extol the virtues of social obligation. Fabians did not simply seek the 'greatest happiness of the greatest number'. They argued that the relief of poverty was a *sine qua non* to the promotion of happiness. This was a fundamental philosophical departure from Benthamite utilitarianism, which informed poor law society and was concerned with the consequences rather than the morality of actions taken by the State.

In ideological terms the Fabians tend to be regarded as socialists, but in many respects they were engaged in reformulating classical republican ideals of citizenship in terms of an inclusive moral community. Moreover, as Cole and Postgate (1961: 423) have observed, they were singularly nationalist in orientation: 'socialism of this sort was so directly based on British conditions as to have about it, inevitably very little that was international, beyond a general sympathy with the parallel assumptions of workers in other countries'. The Fabians rejected revolutionary socialism in favour of evolutionary socialism. They came to diametrically opposite conclusions to the Marxists on the core issue of the future of capitalism. The Marxists argued that capitalism would founder on its inherent contradictions arising out of the relations of production (discussed below). The Fabians believed that 'the problems of production had largely been solved, from which it followed that society could now begin to occupy itself with the infinitely more agreeable problem of distribution' (Lichtheim, 1961: 211). In this regard the Fabians were remarkably prescient in anticipating postmodern society with its emphasis on the consumer.

The Fabians' Anglocentricism subsequently led to the mistaken belief that the institution of the Welfare State was uniquely British. It assumed a national superiority in terms of social progress that belied the facts. Both New Zealand and Sweden had created Welfare States informed by similar social democratic principles before Britain. In the case of Sweden a more elaborate welfare system had been achieved. In reality, Fabianism is a national variant of the European social model that made it a pioneer in the field of social policy until the 1970s (EU, 1996: 30)

Because the Fabians had equated the concepts of welfare collectivism and social obligation, the benign nature of the State has been assumed. Evidence to the contrary has largely been ignored. Mishra (1977: 10) has observed that 'the social and political significance of Bismarck's Welfare State and later Hitler's concept of a people's community in Nazi Germany, has not featured to any great extent on the curriculum of social policy studies in Britain'. Moreover, the historiography of the Welfare State is presented in terms of a progression from barbarism to enlightenment (see Bruce, 1968; Fraser, 1973). This idealist view of history attributes all reform to a combination of altruism and religious sentiment, which, it is argued, incrementally improve the human condition. The genocidal consequences of the application of Victorian social policies during the Great Famine (1845–8) in Ireland are ignored (Powell, 1992: 97–101).

Consistent with their belief in the ideal of progress, the Fabians were strongly influenced by Comtean positivism, which advocated the application of the empirical methods of the natural sciences to the study of social problems with a view to creating 'social physics' or social science. The self-helping activities of friendly societies and the endeavours of philanthropic organisations were increasingly being recognised as unequal to the task of eliminating poverty in a complex industrial society. In this context the use of social statistics in the documentation of poverty became a vital instrument for the social reformer. The poverty surveys of Charles Booth and Seebohm Rowntree, carried out in Britain at the turn of the century and replicated by Stafford in Dublin (1907) and McSweeney in Cork (1914), were seminal as indicators of social progress, epitomising this process. Beatrice Webb, who assisted Booth in his London-based survey, observed that once their social statistics had been published 'the net effect was to give an entirely fresh impetus to the general adoption of the policy of securing to every individual, as the basis of his life and work, a prescribed national minimum of the requisites for efficient parenthood and citizenship' (Webb, 1926: 239).

The achievement of a Welfare State in post-War Britain, the uncontested political formation between 1945 and 1975, represented the fruition of Fabian aspirations. However, the limitations of the British Welfare State were exposed by Brian Abel-Smith and Peter Townsend in their classic 1960s survey, *The Poor and the Poorest*. It mirrored Michael Harrington's parallel study in the United States, entitled *The Other America* (1963), which revealed an underclass largely untouched by the Affluent Society and New Deal social reformism. Cloward and Piven further attacked the New Deal and President Johnson's 1960s Great Society programme in a searing analysis called *Regulating the Poor*, published in 1972. This book equated welfare with social control in a devastating critique of the core values of the welfare society project.

In Ireland, Fabianism in general and the Welfare State in particular received a critical reception at the outset of the post-War era. A debate commenced regarding the desirability of a Welfare State that came to be known as the 'Liberal Ethic controversy'. It involved a collision between traditionalist Catholic values and the secular humanist idiom of the Welfare State. At its crudest it was a contest between Catholic and State power, epitomised by Dr Noel Browne's proposal to introduce socialised health care for mothers and children in 1951, which brought the Inter-Party Government down (Powell, 1992: 253–261).

One of the principal critics of the Welfare State in the Liberal Ethic controversy was the Professor of Philosophy at University College Galway, Fr Felim O'Briain, who caricatured the Welfare State as 'the Silken Tyranny'. Fr O'Briain, in a series of newspaper articles, characterised the Welfare State as 'a variant of the cruder methods of Nazism, Fascism, Communism', and referred to 'Welfare totalitarianism' and 'the dehumanisation that State paternalism is bound to achieve' (*Irish*

Independent, November, 1952).

O'Briain's strictures against the Welfare State were closely in harmony with Catholic social philosophy, which viewed negative State interference (i.e. policing) as permissible but regarded positive State action (i.e. welfare) as unacceptable. This ultramontanist view of the world favoured the principle of subsidiarity, i.e. that the State should be a last resort. From the perspective of traditional Catholic values epitomised by Belloc, the Welfare State was in reality the 'Servile State'.

The departure of Eamonn de Valera from power at the end of the 1950s and his replacement by Sean Lemass opened the way for the modernisation of Irish Society, which commenced in the 1960s. The Catholic Church's view of the Welfare State also changed following the Second Vatican Council in the early 1960s. In an incremental fashion an Irish Welfare State emerged in the 1960s and 1970s and continued to flourish until 1987, when the influence of New Right policies of fiscal rectitude began to be felt in Ireland.

Conservatism and civic virtue

The ideals of civic virtue and social obligation dominated social thought in the Western World between 1900 and 1975. They gave rise to the Welfare State as an antidote to the vagaries of the market and the iniquities of a society based on the principle of acquisitive individualism. Since the mid-1970s inflation, stagnation and external trade imbalances have created new realities. The Welfare State had represented for many a growing civilisation of expectations in which social obligation and civic virtue became synonymous (Elias, 1939; De Swann, 1988).

Classical conservatism, once the most powerful critique of capitalism, does not exist anymore. There is no political movement in the developed world arguing the case for divine right, landed aristocracies and organic society. Capitalism has fundamentally transformed the social, political and economic institutions that dominated Western civilisation for millennia. In its place, it has created a dynamic, materialistic and all-pervasive global culture. All that is left of classical conservatism is a romantic yearning for a world of lost innocence, as is imagined to have existed prior to its transformation by capitalism and its ideological counterpart, liberalism. Burgeoning global capitalism, by curtailing expenditure possibilities, has also undermined the Welfare State as the political solution to societal contradictions.

Economic retrenchment has not only severely restricted the

possibilities for reform, but spawned a neo-conservative movement, advocating a return to the doctrines of classical liberalism, social authoritarianism and the dismantling of the Welfare State. Neo-conservatives charge the Welfare State with responsibility for creating a 'dependency culture', which, it is argued, has led to disincentives both to work and to invest. This new anti-reformist or post-reformist era presents social reformers with a fundamental challenge, which goes to the core of the normative assumptions on which the reformist tradition rests. The 'primitive questions' posed by the influential American neo-conservative social policy analyst, Charles Murray, challenge the concept of civic virtue which has characterised traditional social policy discourse. Murray (1984: 197) openly advocates an antinomian perspective that rejects the notion of civic virtue, enquiring 'why should one person give *anything* to a stranger whose only claim to his help is a common citizenship?'. Marsland (1996: 106), in similar vein, has asserted that 'the most damaging impact of the Welfare State is on the character, motivations and behaviour of individual men and women subjected to its comprehensive expropriation of their capacity for free and independent action, for self-reliance, for enterprising initiative and for moral autonomy'. Like Murray, Marsland (1996: 115) concludes apocalyptically that unless the Welfare State is fundamentally restructured, 'the whole fabric of civilised life in a free society will be threatened'.

Ultimately, the neo-conservative critics of the ideal of social obligation argued that the Welfare State was become counter-productive, creating a dependency culture. Murray (1984) concluded that redistributive welfare strategies are inexorably pushing the poor further into poverty and destabilising the social order. The influence of utilitarian logic and empirical methodology in Murray's work leads to conclusions diametrically opposed to those of social reformers in the Fabian tradition. This critique highlights the ideological vulnerability of the reformist tradition based on the ideal of social obligation. Murray has arguably gone furthest in turning the methodology of the reformist tradition in social policy against itself. He is, however, part of a long tradition of anti-collectivists including Hayek, Friedman and Joseph. The 1980s represented the high-water mark of their influence.

The conservatism of the late 1990s has been tempered by a reassessment, among its more moderate exponents, of the market as a viable basis for social organisation. There is a growing recognition among conservatives that their unqualified espousal of the free market has left them open to the charge of promoting selfishness and endorsing indifference to the plight of the poor. Moreover, the social fracture that has become the legacy of neo-conservative economics has caused a spiralling sense of public angst. The distinguished conservative philosopher, Roger Scruton, has observed in this regard that 'no one doubts the value of economic freedom or the spirit of enterprise; but the exclusive emphasis on these things looks like so much self-serving rhetoric on the part of those whose only interest is profit and whose concern for the community goes no further than the search for customers' (*Observer*, 9 February 1997). Both the French and British General Elections in 1997 constituted a rejection of neo-conservatism, most clearly in France where a highly interventionist Government has been installed.

There is evidence of a resurgence of the civic conservatism originated by Bismarck and Disraeli, which would combine radical tax and welfare reforms with decentralisation and devolution of the State, in a political strategy that would combine free enterprise with a new emphasis on community and social obligation. Clearly, in this civic conservatism, the voluntary sector would be fundamental in defining a civil society that is agreeable to the tenets of conservative philosophy, i.e. profoundly anti-statist.

There must be doubts as to whether civic virtue, notably social obligation, can be sustained in a global market economy, which is by definition antinomian. There are shared global concerns, such as the preservation of the environment and the prevention of war, but these are weak compared with the vested interests of global capital. When society no longer has boundaries, defined by shared values rooted in culture, religion, history and tradition, it is difficult to see how it can maintain cohesion. This is the basic weakness in the conservative position that seeks to look back nostalgically at a past it is undermining by the unleashing of unfettered global market forces. Civic virtue and social obligation, arguably, are not sustainable in an unfettered market society, since such concerns are irrelevant to the pursuit of profit. The only values in the market place are exchange values. At its most extreme, the concern must be that laissez-faire capitalism could lead to increased instability and even social collapse. That is, very properly, the concern of civic conservatives, and that is why they seek to promote civil society within a global market economy.

Critical theory and social policy

Because of the prevailing Fabian consensus around the ideal of social obligation, the normative aspects of the emergent discipline of social policy were neglected in favour of its more empirical preoccupations until the 1970s. George and Wildings' seminal work *Ideology and Social Welfare*, first published in 1976, began the task of mapping out the normative and explanatory theoretical basis of social policy. The following year, Mishra's *Society and Social Policy* not only addressed the theoretical foundations of social policy but sought to compare and contrast its application in capitalist and socialist societies. This application of critical social theory to the analysis of welfare has opened up new horizons for students of social policy. More fundamentally, it has revealed the limits of the Fabian reformist tradition and challenged the normative assumptions of the Welfare State.

The development of a revisionist or critical school of social policy during the 1970s and 1980s has paralleled the crisis in welfare capitalism and the emergence of a postmodern political culture. Marxist and neo-Marxist social thought has been seminal to the critical school of social policy. The relevance of Marxist social theory to the study of social policy has been delineated by Mishra (1977: 68):

> First as a comprehensive theory of society it provides an explanation of the nature of welfare and its development in bourgeois and other societies. Secondly, as a normative theory concerned with the transcendence of capitalism it offers a particular view of problems germane to welfare and their 'definitive' solution.'

Undoubtedly, Marx's thought is fundamental to a socialist critique of welfare. But, since he died in 1883, the Welfare State lay outside his experience and was consequently never directly addressed by him. However, in recent years a large number of social policy analysts and social economists have developed a critique of the Welfare State derived from the core principles of Marx's social theory, notably the Materialist Conception of History and the Labour Theory of Value.

The Marxist theory of historical materialism turned conventional wisdom on its head. It rejected idealism as the motor force in history and replaced it with materialism. The superstructure consisting of the ideological make-up of society (i.e. ideas, morality, culture, etc.) was

41

ultimately determined by economic relations. As Lee and Raban (1988: 11) observed, 'Marxists employed a "catastrophic" theory of history'.

Civic virtue was, therefore, simply a reflection of class interest. Social obligation was impossible in a society based on class conflict. History, for Marx, reflected a struggle between classes through a dialectical process, which would ultimately lead to a proletarian State. Progressively, more modern forms of society replaced older ones. Capitalism replaced the feudal social order, which in turn had replaced ancient society, the successor of Asiatic civilisation. Each civilisation was characterised by a set of property relations that had been successfully challenged by a revolutionary class, thus giving way to a new social order. Marx predicted that the capitalist system in turn would perish as the result of its internal contradictions leading to the emergence of a socialist society based on common ownership.

The internal contradictions of capitalism are explained in the labour theory of value. According to Marx, all economic value derives from labour. Capital has a purely parasitical role in the process of production, creaming off the surplus value of labour, i.e. profit. The capitalist minority, through its monopoly of wealth, forces the worker to sell his labour in return for a subsistence wage, creating an exploitative relationship analogous to that with the slave in ancient society or the serf in medieval society. The essential difference from earlier social formations is that the worker is freed from the bondage of settlement (largely because capitalism requires the mobility of labour) and he enjoys basic human rights arising from the power of organised labour. In a constant battle to maximise profits, capitalists seek to increase productivity through deregulation, cutting wages, extending working hours, automation and redundancy, casualisation of labour or moving to Third World economies where wages are lower. Workers, through the trade union movement, seek to counteract this process and improve working conditions and pay. This leads to an ongoing class war, which crucially affects the social policies and legal decisions of the State according to the relative strengths or weakness of the organised working class at any given point in time. Ultimately, the Marxists claim, Government in capitalist society seeks to protect the rights of property.

According to Marxists, crises in capitalism occur for two reasons. First, through over-accumulation which arises when profit and investment outrun demand, since the latter is constrained by the

42

consumer power of the workers. Marx argued that these crises would become increasingly severe until a terminal stage was reached. Cole and Postgate (1961: 419) observed in this context: 'Herein lies the growing contradictions of capitalism—its tendency to defeat itself by producing more than it allows society the means of consuming, and its tendency, by filling up the world with rival capitalist groups, to destroy its power to get rid abroad of surplus products which cannot be consumed at home'. The Wall Street Crash in 1929 was caused by this factor but it did not bring an end to capitalism, which was reformed by the New Deal and the Welfare State.

Second, according to Marxists, crises in capitalism arise when workers succeed in achieving real wage increases and the expansion of State expenditure on social services—i.e. a measurable degree of social reform. This results in domestic inflation and disinvestment by capitalists in the national economy. As a result, a structural gap develops between revenue and expenditure (as occurred in the 1980s in Ireland), leading to economic retrenchment of unemployment and ultimately, it is hoped, to the return of capital investment.

The Welfare State, according to Marxists, is based on a contradiction. It grants workers social and economic rights in order to bind them to the capitalist system and prevent the threat of revolution, that would create a workers' State. According to Offe (1984: 153), this is the ultimate contradiction in capitalism: 'while capitalism cannot coexist with, neither can it exist without, the Welfare State'. In other words, Marxists believe that in order to maintain social cohesion capitalism promotes civic virtue through the extravagant and potentially ruinous mechanism of the Welfare State.

Marxist critics of the Welfare State have tended to overstate their case, viewing it essentially as doomed by inherent flaws including: (1) ineffectiveness and inefficiency, (2) its repressive nature and (3) the conditioning of a false (ideological) understanding of social and political reality within the working class (Offe, 1984: 154). As Lee and Raban (1988: 108) have put it, 'a definite and quite dramatic tension exists between Marxism as a guide to political practice and Marxism as a body of critical theory'.

Empirical research in Ireland and elsewhere, as noted in Chapter 1, has indicated broad support for public expenditure on pensions, public health insurance and family/child allowances—all entitlements that benefit the majority. Much less popular is welfare expenditure on unemployment and public assistance, which is directed at the minority underclass (Pierson, 1992: 169). None the less, despite the most pessimistic predictions by Marxists, the Welfare State has retained popular support in liberal democratic societies, confounding the logic of their critique. The ultimate problem of the Marxist critique of the Welfare State are what Lee and Raban (1988) describe as the 'theoretical excesses of fundamentalism' conditioned by economic reductionism and functionalist forms of analysis. By discounting democracy as a force for social change, Marxists have severely underestimated the importance of the Welfare State. Marxists ignore the fundamental relationship between democracy and State Welfare. Before democracy there was no State Welfare. The Welfare State is the product of democratic pluralism and the embodiment of modern citizenship.

Postmodernity and social change

What critics of the Welfare State have, however, successfully identified is a structural shift in postmodern society, which has brought the dirigiste model of social democracy into disfavour, because the public no longer perceives it to be self-evidently emancipatory in intent. As Keane (1984: 2), writing in a British context, puts it: 'formerly recognised as the main procedure for limiting the abuse of authoritarian power, democracy becomes the ally of heteronomy, and democratic socialism becomes virtually synonymous with the bureaucratisation of existence with the domains of State and society'.

In Germany, social scientists such as Gadamer, Apel and Habermas have reached similar conclusions. The Irish political commentator, John Waters, eloquently stated the problem of the post-War consensus around the Welfare State:

> The primary impulse of post-War politics in both East and West was to refuse to hand power downwards to people, but instead to invest it in the apparatus of Government at either national or supra-national level. When that power followed the natural urge to expand, it was allowed to expand upwards and outwards, but never down. In both ideological systems, the purpose of Government of economics, of social policy, was not the betterment of people's lives, but the efficient operation of the technology of power. (*Irish Times*, 23 March 1993)

The emergence of social movements and identity politics, based on gender, age, sexuality, disability, etc., questioned the traditional

44

universalist assumptions of redistributionist social policy, which extolled the civic virtues that created the basis for a moral community. It has also challenged the notion of class as the basis for inequality. In postmodern society the uni-dimensional nature of traditional social politics has been challenged by identity politics with a particularistic or fractured definition of inequality.

The politics of recognition is counterpoised to the politics of redistribution. Consequently, distinctive feminist and anti-racist approaches to social policy analysis have emerged as part of the critical school of social policy. In Ireland, Mary Daly's *Women and Poverty*, published in 1989, is a classic exposition of the feminist critique of the Welfare State. Both the Irish Travellers Movement and the Dublin Travellers' Education and Development Group have developed a rich body of anti-racist social policy literature in Ireland. The Disablement Movement and Gay Rights have also found a voice. These new departures in social policy analysis pose major challenges to discourse in a society which has traditionally screened out alternative perspectives. The universalism of the Welfare State is challenged by particularism arising out of the replacement of class-based social inequality by a plethora of social movements, all concerned with the recognition of their identity and attendant rights. The resulting Welfare rights paradigm has challenged the paternalism of the Welfare State and exposed its weaknesses and limitations.

Justice, decency and social obligation

The clash of ideologies between the rampant free market values of the right and the left, fragmented into the traditional social politics of the Welfare State, neo-Marxism and the identity politics of multiculturalism, occludes a deeper problem. There is a crisis of belief in the Welfare State. It is partly due to the declining influence of the radical humanist values, traceable to the Enlightenment, that have shaped it.

A Welfare State reflects not merely the values of a democracy but the image it has of itself as a just and decent society. The Welfare State is based on the ideal of social obligation, in which the entitled citizen has a right to have his or her needs met. Increasingly, this concept has been broadened into a set of rights or expectations that some commentators argue are no longer realisable, creating a pervasive sense of disillusionment with Government. The problem, as Melanie Phillips (1997: 13) has put it, is that in a consumer culture 'rights' have been translated into 'wants'. She holds politicians responsible for this development:

> Politicians have refused to speak the language of priorities essential to all responsible Government. They have refused to exercise political leadership and to stand for a concept of common good. They have treated people not as citizens with reciprocal duties to each other and to their society but as consumers with an inalienable right to obtain whatever they desire. They have created a culture of escalating and never realisable rights which has destroyed social cohesion by setting up competition between interests and eroded the duty to take responsibility for ourselves and our families.

Phillips' critique of the Welfare State is somewhat overstated. It ignores the systematic reduction in expectations and downsizing of the Welfare State that have taken place over the past two decades. None the less, there is an important underlying truth in Phillips' argument: a just society, based on social rights, is not necessarily a decent society. The issue of welfare rights has dominated the debate about the Welfare State in recent decades, to the exclusion of other values, notably the ideal of social obligation. Rawls' influential theory of social justice has given intellectual coherence to this perspective in liberal democratic society. The problem is, however, that the Rawlsian view places rights within a highly individualist context, ignoring the larger communitarian context. Ignatieff (1997: 10) has commented that there is a considerable gap between justice and decency in the Welfare State, which in his view institutionally humiliates its claimant population. As he puts it:

> Indeed the Welfare State makes a practice of recognising the right to relief, but in a humiliating manner. Such humiliations are not casual or accidental. They may be consequent and deliberate, an attempt to discourage the unemployed from claiming what is their due. Justice between tax payers and claimants is often held to require the imposition of some deterrent effect in the way we deliver benefit. The deterrent effect may not be unjust, but it is certainly indecent.

A society that practises institutional humiliation in order to control access to entitlements by linking welfare to the principle of deterrence, based on the practice of humiliation, is the very antithesis of a decent society.

So what can be deduced from the various critiques of the Welfare State? Has it failed? Should it be abolished? Is social obligation achieved only through voluntarism? If one accepts the neo-conservative critique,

46

then civic virtue belongs exclusively to the realms of personal initiative, and the Welfare State has failed and should be abolished. However, neo-conservatives do not argue that there is any obligation to help a stranger (Murray, 1984). Rather, welfare is a matter of personal prudence, moral sentiment and religious virtue, as opposed to social rights or obligations. On the other hand, if one accepts the view of an unqualified welfare rights paradigm as the only basis for social justice, questions arise about the finite nature of resources and the need for a contractual basis for welfare, in which individual citizens also have social obligations towards the community.

How does one resolve this ideological conflict? The New Zealand-based sociologist, Ian Culpitt, has suggested a reassertion of the ideal of social obligation as a way forward. He argues that 'the current welfare rights paradigm has no theory of obligation and has only facilitated the proliferation of need claims' (Culpitt, 1992: 34). According to Culpitt (1992: 46), 'what any defence of the Welfare State must argue is not for a renewal of the moral imperative for individuals to care but that it is the practical recognition of mutual vulnerability that leads to a sense of obligation'. He concludes that 'personal and social obligations that respect individual vulnerabilities are not ultimately moral demands upon the arbitrary beneficence of individuals but social demands that recognise the legitimacy of such vulnerabilities' (Culpitt, 1992: 47). New Zealand, which first introduced the Welfare State in the 1930s, has recently abolished it, leaving the poor to the vagaries of providence.

Culpitt's concept of social obligation is important because it eschews the individual concepts favoured by the welfare rights paradigm and neo-conservatives in favour of a more communitarian view of welfare based on reciprocity. It links justice to decency in defining social obligation. Furthermore, Culpitt's concept of social obligation acknowledges a close interdependence between the individual and society. However, it does not insist that this relationship must be mediated entirely by the State. There is room for welfare pluralism in a society that is both just and decent. In this context, a civilised society that is democratic rather than paternalistic emerges. Moreover, recipients of welfare are the dependants neither of philanthropists or of State bureaucrats, but entitled citizens within a democracy that acknowledges its social obligations.

This removes much of the philosophical basis underpinning the

47

conflict between political partisans. As Culpitt (1992: 36) puts it:

> Much of the clash between left and right depends on the classic dualism of public/private. Both political philosophies attempt to prove that their ontological view is not only superior but is the only possible one. However, there are systemic connections between the idea of private and public worlds and the 'meaning' of this ontological division resides outside the rigidity of the internal logic of the separate arguments.

We can therefore conclude that the basis for taking the Welfare State project forward into the new millennium depends on moving the argument beyond the welfare rights issue that has dominated late-twentieth-century debate, but not through the systematic erosion or abolition of these rights: rather through the renegotiation of the social contract in a manner that acknowledges both rights and obligations based on a recognition of shared vulnerabilities and common citizenship. The EU Comité des Sages (1996: 45) has made an important contribution in this regard, advising against 'handing down rights from on high: Rights should be evolved in a democratic process based on the principles of active citizenship'. This wise advice links entitled citizenship to active citizenship, rights to obligations and ultimately places trust in the people. The EU Comité des Sages (1996: 45–46) also comments that 'the process by which rights evolve is almost as important as their content: rights which are jointly worked out by a democratic process over an adequate period of time will be more readily respected than those formulated by experts'. The Comité des Sages (1996) concludes that 'citizenship is not merely a collection of rights: it is also a way of living, of recognising one's obligations to others, of participating in society, through a multiplicity of relationships with its members'.

Conclusion

In the reconstructed reality of postmodern society, the challenge of social policy is to respond reflexively to changing needs and demands. The challenge to universalist welfare based on social obligation, common citizenship and human rights is manifest. If particularism in the shape of identity politics and burgeoning social movements, including the neo-conservative movement, is to be the shape of things to come, where does that leave civic virtue? Is it possible to have a civil society in a polarised and fragmented social order? This is the great social, political and intellectual challenge of postmodernity. The concept of social obligation based on shared vulnerabilities has been suggested as a basis for civic virtue in postmodern society. However, it is not unproblematic given the difficulties in maintaining civic trust in a deeply fragmented and polarised society, where the fate of voluntarism has become entangled with the coercive institution of workfare.

Chapter 3: Civic Trust, Citizenship and Voluntarism

Economic and social trends in recent years have undermined civic trust significantly by increasing the numbers of those marginalised or excluded from the mainstream of society. This process, which has been graphically characterised as 'the Brazilianisation of the West', entails increasingly ostentatious forms of exclusion with groups of people living in severe poverty and under barely life-sustaining conditions — in and from the garbage of 'normal' society. Unemployment has broken the link for many with the external world of work. A lack of child-care facilities makes it difficult for women to participate in the workforce in the first instance. These problems are compounded in certain areas, such as the peripheral housing estates, where marginalised groups are concentrated and where physical isolation and the sparseness of community facilities reinforce social exclusion. Minority groups, such as Travellers, HIV/AIDS victims, drug addicts, refugees and migrant workers experience the sharp end of exclusion in a growing climate of social tensions exacerbated by the increasing emphasis on ethnicity in defining citizenship. Social exclusion represents a qualitative change in the way people relate to each other, manifested by ever-widening inequalities, spiralling levels of violence and a breakdown in social solidarity. It involves a crisis of civic trust because it breeds a popular lack of confidence in the social order.

Trust is the basis of an inclusive society. The Green Paper on the Community and Voluntary Sector (Department of Social Welfare, 1997: 25) observes in this regard that:

> It is important to create a culture and society which respects the autonomy of the individual. In such a society, individuals are given the opportunity to realise their potential and to take potential for themselves and others. This means creating a climate which supports individuals and groups to make things happen rather than have things happen to them. Such a culture respects diversity and community solidarity. Interdependence is built on trust and dialogue . . . All people, but especially those who are at present excluded, must be facilitated to participate in dialogue about problems, policy solutions and programme implementation. For dialogue to take place

50

with Government agencies, officials must ensure that their is openness and trust and that there is flexibility towards new interactive ways of responding to issues and concerns of those who are excluded.

What is meant by the term 'social exclusion'? The association of poverty with a more divided society has led to the broader concept of social exclusion, which refers not only to material deprivation but also to the inability of the poor to exercise fully their social, cultural and political rights as citizens. The concept of social exclusion has become particularly influential in European Commission policy circles: for example, the Green Paper on Social Policy (Commission of European Communities, 1993: 551) argues that 'social exclusion . . . by highlighting the flaws in the social fabric . . . suggests something more than social inequality, and, concomitantly, carries with it the risk of a dual and fragmented society'. Fragmentation is compounded by social polarisation dividing society into haves and have nots, disconnecting the excluded minority from the rest of society. As *Partnership 2000* (1997: 17) (the basis for Irish public policy between 1997 and 2000) put it:

> Social exclusion can be succinctly described as cumulative marginalisation from production (unemployment), from consumption (income poverty), from social networks (community, family and neighbours), from decision making and from an adequate quality of life. Social exclusion is one of the major challenges currently facing Irish society. To minimise or ignore this challenge would not only result in an increase in social polarisation, which is in itself unacceptable, but also an increase in all the attendant problems such as poor health, crime, drug abuse and alienation, which impose huge social and economic costs on our society.

The purpose of this chapter is to examine changing values and practices informing social policy in the late twentieth century and to pose three questions. First, are we reverting to classical poor law forms in social provision as market values once again became dominant? Second, what are the implications of these changes for the definition and meaning of citizenship in postmodern society? Third, is workfare undermining voluntarism by fundamentally violating its value base in free choice?

Welfare and citizenship

Citizenship can be defined in T. H. Marshall's classic formulation as consisting of 'a three legged stool'. First, there are fundamental civil rights such as freedom of speech, thought and religious toleration;

51

equality before the law, the due process of the justice system, the right to conclude contracts as equals—the rule of law in its broadest sense. Second, there are basic political rights including the right to vote, form political parties and contest elections—democratic pluralism in essence. Third, there are basic social rights: 'the whole range from the right to a modicum of economic welfare and security to the right to share to the full the social heritage and to live the life of a civilised being according to the standards of the prevailing society' (Marshall, 1973: 72).

The development of social citizenship rights, according to the Marshallian thesis, is the product of class struggle incrementally promoting an increasingly egalitarian society for the majority. The erosion of traditional social inequalities has served to compress income differentials for the working population at both ends of the spectrum to create an increasingly popular and universalistic culture and to establish firm links between education and occupation based on the meritocratic ideal. A universal status of social citizenship has emerged in democratic pluralist societies encompassing the majority working population.

In this regard, the Scandinavian social scientist, Esping-Andersen (1990: 21), in the tradition of T. H. Marhsall, shares the view that 'Social citizenship constitutes the core idea of the Welfare State . . . But the concept of social citizenship also involves social stratification: one's status as a citizen will compete with, or even replace, one's class position'. Esping-Andersen is essentially endorsing the view that social rights have led to a breaking down of social class inequalities based on labour market positions. According to his decommodification theory, when social rights are added to civil and political rights society moves away from treating people as commodities or things, to a consideration of their essential humanity. Esping-Andersen (1990: 11) has thus reopened an old debate: 'the central question, not only for Marxism but for the entire contemporary debate on the Welfare State, is whether and under what conditions, the class divisions and social inequalities produced by capitalism can be undone by parliamentary democracy'.

Paradoxically, the emergence of egalitarian citizenship as the direct product of class struggle has led to a decline of the latter. As the working class secured direct influence over the State, transforming it into the Welfare State, working-class allegiance to its institutions was ensured. Struggle for control over the economy (in socialist parlance the 'means of production') has abated and the working class have become clients of the

Welfare State. Corporatist structures have emerged within the Welfare State leading to agreements between social partners (Government, labour and business) in 'the national interest'. The *Programme for National Recovery* (PNR), 1987, the *Programme for Economic and Social Progress* (PESP), 1990, the *Programme for Competitiveness and Work* (PCW), 1994, and *Partnership 2000*, 1997 epitomise the welfare corporatist process in action in Ireland. The voluntary sector has been drawn into this symbiotic relationship, blurring distinctions between it and the State (see below).

The significance of social citizenship is that democratic participation is based on the citizen's relationship not with the means of production but with the means of distribution—with the Welfare State rather than the market economy. This is, as already suggested, essentially a clientelist relationship between the citizen and the State. Within such an arrangement political parties vie with each other for the citizen's electoral support. In this political order the State has achieved hegemony through regulating the relationship between labour and business and the redistributive systems involving taxation and social welfare benefits.

The term 'status' has been widely interpreted, in this context, as meaning a set of legal entitlements from the State for minimum social and economic standards. Minimum standards are understood in the late twentieth century in terms of lifestyle and social consumption rather than working conditions—the traditional priority of the labour movement. There is widespread agreement that social citizenship rights in contemporary Western developed societies have conferred on the majority of the population access to complex status items in both the public and private spheres. In the public sphere in Ireland these include above all the right to home ownership (enjoyed by 80% of the population) but also State-guaranteed pension rights, high-quality State-subsidised health care and increasing access to second-level education (80% of the population) and a rapidly expanding and modernising third-level sector. In the private sphere, access to privatised transportation, foreign holidays, electronically mediated mass entertainment and technologised leisure equipment are considered basic necessities of a normal lifestyle. However, these gains in the quality of life for the individual have been achieved at considerable cost to the social. Traditional social rights (e.g. to education and training, health care, work and fair conditions of work and pay, a minimum income in the event of

53

unemployment, a retirement pension) have been eroded by privatisation and public expenditure cuts and a lowering of standards. A new generation of social rights (e.g. to environmental protection, sustainable use of resources, choice of work and social inclusion) have been neglected.

Postmodern society and the underclass

In postmodern society the exclusion of the underclass poses the ultimate challenge. The inclusion of a substantial section of the working class in the consumer society has served to fragment its traditional solidarity. An excluded underclass has emerged defined by its prescribed status as supplicant in the Welfare State. The emergence of what has come to be called 'the underclass' is a potent manifestation of the importance of productive relations in determining class solidarity. The underclass is differentiated from the majority population by age, gender and ethnicity, as well as employment status. A thumbnail demography of the Irish underclass according to a multitude of studies reveals a population marginalised on the periphery of society consisting of the unemployed, lone (usually female) parents, the disabled and elderly, as well as small farmers. As already noted, beyond these groups exist several minority groups which experience social exclusion in its most extreme form, including Travellers, people suffering from HIV/AIDS, drug abusers, refugees and migrant workers. The fact that they are usually excluded from poverty studies exacerbates their social exclusion. (Gan, 1996: 151) has suggested that the term 'undercaste' might more accurately describe this 'population of such low status as to be shunned by the rest of society'.

In 1988 an Economic and Social Research Institute (ESRI) report on poverty, sponsored by the Combat Poverty Agency, which was the largest poverty study undertaken in the history of the State, concluded that a minimum of one in three people are living on inadequate incomes in Ireland. The ESRI research also concluded that the situation was deteriorating: the numbers of people in poverty increased at a faster pace in the 1980s than in the 1970s (Combat Poverty Agency: 1988). A follow-up study based on the 1994 Living in Ireland survey demonstrated that the poor were not as poor as they had been in 1987, but that the number of those who fell below the poverty line remained much the same (Combat Poverty Agency, 1996). The Irish situation reflects global trends towards increasing inequality, sometimes referred to as the 'Silent

Depression', with the poorest fifth of the world's population sharing on average little more than 5% of wealth, while the richest fifth possess 40%–60%. In the USA, incomes for high school drop-outs have declined by 23.3% since 1973, high school graduates have experienced a 17% drop in income and even some college students (who have not studied to degree level) have had a fall in income of 7.3%. At the other end of the social spectrum, 1% of the nation's richest households have 40% of the country's wealth (Cohen: 1995).

Postmodernity has brought with it a sharp decline in the traditional employment base of the working class in the manufacturing industries. This has displaced a substantial section of the workforce, resulting in unemployment or low-paid (often casual) employment in the expanding business services sector, e.g. catering, retailing and cleaning services. While it is difficult to share fully Gorz's (1982) view that the traditional working class has been replaced by a 'non-class' of 'non-proletarians', the impact of post-industrialisation in dividing the working class is irrefutable. It is also correct to argue that the name 'underclass' is a misnomer in terms of defining the condition of the socially excluded in postmodern society. As Dahrendorf observes:

> The underclass does not pose a class problem. Technically, the name, underclass is wrong. Classes are conflict groups based on common interest conditions within a framework of relations . . . The underclass on the contrary is a mere victim. It is unlikely to organise and defend the many similar yet not really common interests of its members .

It is therefore not surprising that the 1980s witnessed a reopening of the debate on the nature of citizenship and a reassertion of its duties and obligations at the expense of rights and entitlements. The implications for the idea of citizenship has led Dahrendorf (1994: 13) to comment that 'there may be a case for emphasising obligations as well as rights, even for a more sparing definition of citizenship rights, but once they lose their unconditional quality, the door is open not just for the invisible hand of the market (which can be benevolent) but above all for the visible hand of rulers who tell people what to do when'. In the case of minority groups, who experience social exclusion at its most extreme (Travellers, HIV/AIDS victims, drug addicts, etc.), Dahrendorf's point has particular resonance.

Exclusion and desert

The distinguished Irish social policy commentator, liberation theologian and redoubtable poverty crusader, Fr Sean Healy (1990: 35-36 commenting on the exclusion of the underclass in 1992, observed that:

> Exclusion is experienced in many ways. If you are excluded it means your opinion is not sought and it doesn't count. In fact you are not expected to have an opinion, rather you are encouraged to trust the opinion of the shapers of society. Ultimately it is not only the feeling but the reality of powerlessness.

He continued:

> When you are one of the excluded, politicians and policy-makers can ignore you without fear of censure or loss of position. If your rights are infringed, the avenues of redress are very few and haphazard. Since society fears excluded groups you are always suspect — guilty until proven innocent.

Fr Healy concluded:

> Generally speaking poverty is the companion of exclusion. People on low incomes have a struggle even to provide the necessary food, clothing and heat. They are not simply 'less comfortable' than everyone else — they have shorter lives, sicker children, babies which are more likely to die in infancy.

In this searing analysis of the condition of the underclass, a minority group denied meaningful participation in citizenship and discriminated against by the majority clearly emerges. The cause of this profound social inequality belongs manifestly to the sphere of political economy, since the exclusion of the underclass derives in the first instance, as Fr Healy suggests, from their poverty. Exclusion from income and welfare is closely linked to exclusion from broader citizenship rights, such as the right to justice and participation.

Poverty campaigners have been sustained by the belief that public opinion is firmly on the side of the poor and that this factor will in the long run lead to the policy changes necessary to abolish poverty. In this regard they may be unduly optimistic. Attitudes towards poverty in Ireland are in fact complex and in some respects contradictory. An MRBI poll published on 18 October 1988 in the *Irish Times* indicated that 66% of the population favoured a tax rise to help the poor. This poll suggested that Irish public opinion has been, in general, favourably disposed to the poor. But this is an oversimplification. A 1984 ESRI survey carried out by Davis, Grube and Morgan revealed that over 80% of the respondents attributed poverty to fatalistic causes, which suggest it is beyond the competence of the State to abolish it. Furthermore, 57% agreed that 'lack of ambition is at the root of poverty' and 53% agreed that 'the majority of people on the dole have no interest in getting a job'. The latter findings indicate a severe lack of sympathy towards the plight of the poor.

In reality, attitudes towards poverty have changed fundamentally in postmodern society, redefining citizenship in terms of duties and obligations rather than the Marshallian construct of social, as well as civil and political, rights. This redefinition of citizenship in terms of classical values has been associated with the political reassertion of market values. It has legitimated substantial cuts in social expenditure in Ireland between 1987 and 1992, in the interests of fiscal rectitude. A more lasting legacy of fiscal rectitude is likely to be the consequent reconceptualisation of poverty in terms of desert, dividing the poor into 'deserving' and 'undeserving' groups based on a moral economy of conduct. Fiscal and moral rectitude have consequently become reflexively connected.

Goodin (1988: 279) has summarised the critique of the Welfare State propounded by exponents of ethical notions of moral desert:

> In its most extreme form, then, the new New Right indictment of the Welfare State in terms of moral deserts holds that the tax transfers system as a whole is just one big informal machine for taking from the deserving and giving to the undeserving. What people have properly earned in the market is taken from them in taxes. It is transferred to welfare recipients who, at least have done virtually nothing to earn these benefits and who, at worst may have come to their present plight through some misconduct of their own and thus be powerfully undeserving of either sympathy or social assistance.

Postmodern society is therefore a world where social morality and economic productivity are closely intertwined – often mirror images of each other. The choice is to be a 'wealth creator' or a wage labourer, with wealth being allocated according to the classical principle of desert, which characterised the Victorian era. Those who are not 'wealth creators' or wage labourers are assigned to the underclass and treated according to their supposed deserts in a value system where the unproductive are regarded as socially and economically useless.

The determination of desert is linked to the concept of dependency. There is a widespread acceptance that the sick, aged and children deserve social support, though how much or what form it takes (i.e.

institutions or in the community) has been debated over many years. A less tolerant attitude is taken towards the unemployed and lone parents who have children born out of wedlock.

This growing emphasis on desert has involved greater reliance on means-tested benefits, considered inferior to 'as of right' benefits for several reasons. Applicants are required to submit themselves to a detailed examination that includes not only their financial status but also, due to the rules of eligibility, many aspects of their private lives and personal behaviour, e.g. the cohabitation rule. For many the constant requirement to establish their desert, as opposed to their right, as claimants is intrusive, demeaning and stigmatising. Moreover, as Twine (1994: 97) points out:

> A means-tested benefit cannot provide a social right of citizenship because it threatens the integrity of the 'self'. This is because the processes attached to proving you are deserving of means-tested benefits are processes of social exclusion. The stigma attached to means-tested benefits threatens not only the applicants' 'sense of self', but also their ability to function as normal human beings.

The plight of the Travelling population highlights a darker side of the new social morality in contemporary Ireland. The Travellers are treated as people without desert. Accordingly, they are denied the right to halting sites and are persecuted under the vagrancy laws. Social prejudice reinforces the administration of the vagrancy laws, creating a system of apartheid between the Travellers and the majority population. The administration of the social welfare system similarly discriminates against the travelling population, implying that their attitude towards the benefit system is characterised by moral turpitude. This leaves the system open to the charge of institutional racism. Neil Crowley (1993: 23) of the Dublin Traveller Education and Development Group, has commented in this context that:

> The Traveller culture and way of life is not recognised and resourced by the institutions of our racist society. This has real consequences for the Traveller community that are of devastating proportions. Racism is a form of social exclusion.

Workfare and voluntarism

The reconceptualisation of poverty in terms of poor law values has had profound implications for both the Welfare State and the voluntary sector. Welfare, in some societies, is no longer perceived as a basic right in civil society, where long-term structural unemployment has eroded the right to work. In the context of mass unemployment a growing emphasis on duties of citizenship has had tangible outcomes not only in terms of major cuts in welfare expenditure and changes in eligibility criteria but also in transforming the citizens' claim to social rights into a requirement to work in return for welfare—*workfare*. According to its advocates workfare, not welfare, should be the norm for the 'undeserving' poor. It is contended by these critics of welfare (as noted in Chapter 2) that the poverty of the underclass is essentially the product of idleness and fecklessness, which are reinforced by dependency. In this new moral economy of conduct a very traditional remedy is prescribed in terms of workfare. What does workfare entail in practice?

Workfare is a coercive requirement imposed on recipients of welfare benefits, originally in the USA, encompassing able-bodied adults under sixty years of age including women with dependent children over six years of age. The inclusion of women with dependent children represents a growing hostility towards lone parents in the developed world. Workfare involves performing work assignments at the minimum wage for a number of hours each week equal to the value of welfare benefits received. Participants in workfare schemes are not considered regular employees and do not acquire employee status or benefits other than workman's compensation. Their assignments are not considered regular jobs. They receive no additional pay. In 1996 President Clinton signed the Welfare Bill that abolished the right to welfare and replaced it with workfare, controversially overturning the New Deal, established in the 1930s as the basis of the American Welfare State. Mr Gordon Brown, the Chancellor of the Exchequer in the 'New Labour' Government elected in Britain in May 1997, declared in similar vein, 'I am interested in developing a Welfare State built around the work ethic' (*Observer*, 11 May 1997). He was referring in particular to Labour's welfare to work scheme for Britain's young unemployed.

In essence, workfare in its classical form (now widely adopted in the United States) replaces the right to welfare and defines the claimant as a miscreant who must be punished rather than helped. Workfare, therefore, is arguably simply another phase in a long line of coercive tactics which have been employed against the poor in the same tradition as the anti-begging statues, backed by whipping and the stocks, in the

14th century and the Dickensian workhouses of the 19th century. This is why workfare has been dubbed 'the new Poor Law'. In Western Europe, according to the Netherlands Platform for Welfare Affairs (NPWA), workfare has taken a less classical form. Public sector employment has been reduced and replaced by job pools and other variants on the workfare theme; consequently, normal jobs are being replaced by second-rate jobs: in the interests of economy, financial responsibilities are shifted, without calculating the consequences in terms of unemployment and social exclusion (NPWA, 1995: 8–9). The NPWA (1995: 9) has concluded that these workfare schemes are likely to have serious social consequences:

> There is a real danger that the twilight zone of second rate jobs and badly paid atypical work will be extended and that a large part of the social services will be manned from within this twilight zone. A twilight zone where people, unable to get work in the regular labour market, will have no choice but to accept a placement. To us this does not seem a very attractive prospect, because it will sustain and legitimise the division of society.

It is not wholly surprising that the idea of workfare is beginning to take root in Ireland, through programmes such as Community Employment (CE schemes), based on a secondary labour market. Admittedly such schemes are voluntary in Ireland, as in other European countries, in marked contradistinction to the USA. But there is an essential linkage between work and welfare, and a blurring of the boundaries between compulsion and consent. In practice, many claimants feel that they have little option but to participate as dutiful citizens.

Workfare (even in the modified form it has taken in Europe) promises to sharpen social divisions further by removing welfare entitlement from the poor, their most meaningful claim to social rights and an essential prerequisite for social citizenship. Moreover, as the respected American social scientists, Frances Fox Piven and Richard Cloward (1985) have pointed out in their book, *The New Class War*, workfare envisages a form of economic apartheid typical of pre-democratic societies. Undoubtedly, the development of long-term work schemes for the unemployed has created a degrading alternative to the right to work in the primary labour market. It has opened up a disturbing fissure in society, which is arguably not compatible with citizenship, since it excludes a significant proportion of the population from meaningful participation as citizens.

Workfare is one of the most troubling issues that has ever faced the voluntary sector. It poses a variety of fundamental challenges, both practical and philosophical. Many voluntary organisations participate in workfare schemes because of funding and/or labour shortages. Indeed, the survival of the voluntary sector may increasingly depend on workfare.

Based on the results of the UCC survey, 2% of the adult population are employed by a voluntary organisation—many as part of Government employment schemes (see Chapter 6 for a more extensive treatment of these results). Detailed analysis of this subject in Chapter 6 highlights an important part of the nature of the relationship between the voluntary sector and the State in contemporary Ireland. Depending on one's political perspective, Community Employment (CE) schemes can represent either the enforcement of a workfare model with a coercive ethos or the representation of responsible citizenship. Useful comparisons can be made with other European countries, where there is a commitment to enforced citizen participation in either the armed forces or the voluntary sector. The situation, as already noted, is even more stark in the United States where there is no welfare without a workfare placement, which is frequently located in the voluntary sector.

Workfare is undoubtedly fraught with moral and political hazards for the voluntary sector. It poses a fundamental threat to the basic ethic of voluntarism, relations between professional staff, volunteers and CE workers and, ultimately, public support for voluntary agencies. It violates the basis of civic trust inherent in the volunteer's engagement with the community, since it is enforced rather than spontaneous participation. Altruism is in danger of being replaced by coercion and decency by degradation.

The basic ethic of voluntarism is to contribute by personal choice, without wage or salary, a service to an individual, group or community. Both society and volunteer are enriched by the giving of time and commitment and the gaining of esteem, personal satisfaction and, often, new skills. Workfare seeks to capitalise on the spirit of voluntarism by blurring the boundaries between voluntary community commitment and compulsion. The conflation of workfare and voluntarism has the potential to devalue voluntary activity and create negative images of voluntarism, in the public mind and among other volunteers. Given the widespread practice of demonising social welfare recipients, it is unlikely that volunteers would wish to be confused with this group—their underclass and outcast status underlines the point.

Workfare also poses a threat for the position of paid professional employees in voluntary agencies by offering free labour as an alternative. Equally, for the workfare recipient there is the issue of exploitation arising from doing similar work to paid employees, without similar remuneration or rights. Paid employees are placed in the invidious position of assessing the performance of workfare participants. They may not be qualified to do this. Furthermore, they may have ethical dilemmas about being drawn into the 'policing system' of the Welfare State.

Moreover, the voluntary sector leaves itself open to the accusation of colluding with Government in downloading responsibility from the State. This neatly fits in with current trends in social policy geared towards the promotion of subsidiarity. The principle of subsidiarity means that the smallest social unit should be the first source of support, starting with the family and working up through the community and voluntary organisations to the State, as a last resort. In this manner Governments use the voluntary sector to shore up deficiencies in State provision. But it does not need to be this way. The National Anti-Poverty Strategy (Department of Social Welfare, 1997) has suggested an alternative vision but it remains to be seen whether its strategy will be adopted by the Government that was elected in June 1997.

Conclusion

In postmodern society, T. H. Marshall's 'three legged stool of citizenship' has become unbalanced. The primacy of market values has turned people into commodities to be discarded through a process of social exclusion. The emancipatory impetus that social rights conferred on citizenship during the twentieth century is consequently under threat. The capacity of the bottom third of the population to participate has been effectively removed. As Twine (1994: 105) puts it:

Citizens require social resources, health and education not only for economic efficiency but also to participate effectively in furthering their own and other people's civil and political rights, to further their life projects . . . without this approach society continually faces the risk that the social exclusion of apparent minorities may lead to the situation in Nazi Germany or to 'ethnic cleansing' as in Bosnia-Herzegovina. It is always possible to apply a categorisation to anyone so as to identify them as a minority for social exclusion. Social exclusion was used as a powerful form of sanction and punishment under the New Poor Law in nineteenth century Britain, and we have lost our sensitivity to its power in the twentieth century.

So what is the alternative? There is no panacea, but there certainly is an alternative, more socially inclusive approach which involves a number of key elements. First, Irish society needs to change its language and ideas regarding the underclass in general, which are currently unduly influenced by the 'winners and losers' philosophy of the market place. It must discover an idiom which unites rather than divides the country, generating a climate of civic trust and social cohesion. To date, Government has failed to find an idiom to engage the imagination of the country in its present perplexed and angry mood. The word 'economic' with its accompanying incomprehensible vocabulary, needs to be replaced by 'society', a word with a recognisable everyday moral dimension that suggests concern at a human level. By 'society' is meant the supra-individual element in social life: what Durkheim called 'representations collectives', consisting of collective sentiments and beliefs, which are necessary to explain the authority of imperative rules and beliefs.

The Church, which has played such a powerful (and often controversial) role in forging a moral community in Ireland, has a very important role to play in this process. Liberation theologians, most notably the Conference of Major Religious Superiors, have pointed the way. They are undoubtedly the most effective poverty lobbyists in contemporary Ireland. It is to be hoped that their episcopal superiors will follow the example set by their courageous advocacy of the cause of the poor, which has the powerful authenticity of genuine moral conviction. However, for the Hierarchy this would be to acknowledge the need for the articulation of a civic morality, a challenge which presents the Irish Church with an awkward dilemma in terms of its unyielding adherence to traditional moral discourse, largely focusing on individual behaviour and sexual mores.

Second, the exclusion of the underclass should be addressed by the development of participatory democratic structures at grass-roots community level, which empower the poor. Unless there is a sense of involvement in decision-making, the alienation of the underclass will continue to fester. Ultimately, the exclusion of the underclass raises questions about social justice in a democracy as a prerequisite for participation in citizenship: a fully developed view of social justice has

63

yet to take root in Ireland, though the 'just society' concept has been around since the 1960s. Fr Sean Healy, of the Conference of Major Religious Superiors, has frankly spoken out on this issue (*Irish Times*, 24 September 1992), warning of the 'underclass revolt' unless the exclusion from the democratic process is ended. While Fr Healy probably overestimates the revolutionary potential of the underclass, there is a serious potential threat to public order and social solidarity.

Third, the voluntary sector, through its espousal of the value of civic participation, also has a key role to play in an increasingly secular society. However, the growing confusion between workfare and voluntarism threatens to violate the basic ethic on which the latter rests. The voluntary sector is at a crossroads in terms of its role and direction. Will it allow itself to be exploited by the State, as the latter downloads its responsibilities for social service provision? The growing co-operation between the voluntary sector and the State threatens to blur traditional distinctions, which could ultimately compromise the integrity of the former and drive away the potential pool of volunteers. The voluntary sector needs to take a hard look at its relationship both with 'the social' and with the State, if it is to have a healthy future.

Chapter 4: Politics, Voluntarism and Community

The French social commentator, Donzelot has addressed the relationship between voluntarism and the State (1980: 54), and concluded (1980:55) that:

> philanthropy in this case is not to be understood as a naively apolitical term signifying a private intervention in the sphere of so-called social problems, but must be considered as a deliberate depolitising strategy for establishing public services and facilities at a sensitive point midway between private initiative and the State.

The purpose of this chapter is to examine the role of voluntarism in the context of changing social values. First the relationship between charity and secular values and the emergence of scientific charity are examined, then the role of the Catholic Church in voluntary provision is analysed. The influence of communitarianism is addressed in the context of progress, and the role of community in postmodern Irish society is considered.

Charity, theodicy and secular values

Charity defines the care of the poor as a Christian duty. In its idealised form charity is presented as an individualistic and altruistic act, as a private affair between two parties, the benefactor and the beneficiary. In reality, charity in the modern era, in sharp contrast to the Middle Ages when it had a genuine religious currency, represents a collective response to the existence of poverty in the wider social interest. Since the seventeenth century, secular values have informed charity discourse. De Swann (1988: 23) has observed in this regard that:

> charity was a form of altruistic behaviour par excellence: the sacrificing of money or goods for the sake of others; moreover, it was a form of action that profited not only the receivers, but also the collectivity of possessors as a whole. While this beneficence may therefore be conceived of as a bilateral relation between the giver and receiver, it must also be understood in the context of collective action on the part of the providers, for the sake of collective interests, such as defence against threats and the maintenance of

labour reserves.

Alms-giving had primarily devolved on the monasteries in medieval Ireland. Bradshaw (1974: 221) has concluded that 'there is clear-cut evidence that while the monasteries were in decline economically and spiritually from the second half of the fifteenth century, their apostolate for charity was being taken over by others'. Commentators have detected a similar decline in charitable activity throughout Europe which has been associated not only with the Reformation but also with the rise of capitalism. It has been argued that the combined influence of these two forces undermined medieval ethics, 'wealth lost its mark of sinfulness, and the idea of voluntary generosity towards the poor as absolution for the sin involved in wealth became meaningless' (Rusche and Kirchheimer, 1939: 36). Charity, apart from evangelical activities, ceased to be associated with institutional religion in the early modern world. Catholic Ireland was no exception to the secularisation of charity, even though the religious have continued to play a uniquely powerful role in the provision of social services (see below).

The 10th Charles c I put Irish charity on a legal footing analogous to the 1601 English Statute on Charitable Uses, the 43rd Elizabeth I c IV Brady (1976: 199) has observed in reference to the import of this development on the character of Irish charity that 'in the post-Reformation period the practice of charity lost what had been its almost exclusively religious connotation and arguably, the need to define charity was inevitably consequent on its growing secularisation'. This process of secularisation involved the delimitation of appropriate causes for charitable support which reflected the main areas of social concern at the time, though the justificatory rhetoric of philanthropic discourse was retained.

In the early nineteenth century Ireland, the poor depended to a large degree on the charity of the rich for their survival. Equally, the rich depended on the docility of the poor for theirs. Paradoxically, as De Swann (1988: 14) has observed, 'a moral order that encompasses the poor, whom it must persuade of the rightness of property, in justifying their exclusion also establishes their claim to part of the surplus'. The institution of charity in early nineteenth century Ireland existed in this moral paradox and was justified by contemporaries by reference to theodicy, a word coined by the German philosopher, Leibniz, in 1710.

The theory of theodicy, in theological terms, asserts God's justice in the creation of the world. Theodicy seeks to reconcile the fact of evil with the existence of a benevolent God. The Reverend Thomas Malthus, who combined the clerical role with the pursuit of the laws of political economy and demography, discussed the concept of theodicy in his *Essay on the Principles of Population*, published in 1798. He argued the case for a theology of scarcity: 'the Supreme Being has ordained, that the earth shall not produce food in great quantities, till much preparatory labour and ingenuity has been exercised upon its surface', (Malthus, 1798: 360). The Malthusian ethic attributes an inherent indolence and sensuality to humanity which inevitably leads to distress. As Dean (1991: 90) puts it, 'the Malthusian ethic amounts to a life and death choice for the poor: to obey or to transgress the dictates of the laws which are essential to divine providence, to choose a particular ascetic form of life or to perish'. Theodicy provided a theological justification for the limitation of charity to the 'deserving' poor, i.e. those disabled by age and infirmity from working, as well as children.

The rich in early modern Ireland, like their European counterparts, did not envisage a liberal distribution of charity to the poor. As Lis and Soly (1979: 195) have put it, 'the charity of the elites centred almost exclusively on the respectable poor: children and the aged, sick and lame'. The impotent poor were differentiated from the 'able-bodied' poor, the former being considered deserving of assistance and the latter of punishment. As early as 1691, Sir William Petty (1691: 78) had enunciated this distinction:

> I further observe, that if there be naturally but 2,000 impotents in Ireland, and that 50 shillings per annum doth maintain the poorer sort of people; it follows that £8,000 per annum would amply maintain all the impotents of Ireland, if well applied. For other beggars . . . are probably but the faults and defects of Government and discipline.

There was a clear distinction between the 'deserving' and the 'undeserving' poor in the mind of contemporaries. Arthur Dobbs (1729: 46), Surveyor General of Ireland, acknowledged a similar distinction between the impotent and able-bodied poor in terms of desert, but noted that the former were 'often left without relief . . . because they stroll about with the others, where it can't be known who are the real objects of compassion'. He concluded that the impotent poor 'ought to be deemed equally cheats with the others' since they gave encouragement to the able-bodied poor to 'join them and propagate a race of thieves and robbers'. Dobbs (1729: 45) attempted to elaborate on his charge regarding the fraudulent nature of mendicancy:

> It is not very easy to give details of the several arts and stratagems they use, to induce the opulent and industrious to be charitable to them. They appear in various forms, mostly affected, or brought upon them by particular management; as blind, lame, dumb, distorted, with running sores, pretended fits, and other disorders. They frequently pretend to loss by fire, or to have numerous families lying sick. They exercise the greatest barbarities upon children, either their own or those they pick up, by blinding them, or breaking and disjointing their limbs when they are young, to make them objects of compassion and charity. Not to mention their debauchery to the girls when grown up; who go about big-bellied, pretending their husbands are sick, and they have to maintain them. Nor the robberies, debauchery and drunkenness that is to be found among them in their merry meetings. And to sum up all, imagine the most complicated scene of wickedness in low life, and it will be found among them.

Dobb's harsh view of mendicant poor reflects the prevalent viewpoint of the rich that indiscriminate charity was positively harmful to the fabric of society (Rusche and Kirchheimer, 1939: 35). An unyielding moralism based on the work ethic had become the ideological hallmark of charity in the early modern world. The thrust of Dobbs' observations on the poor also conferred on them a common deviant status belying the distinction between impotent and able-bodied.

The uncompromising rigidity of Dobbs' position helps explain the absence of a statutory system of poor relief. But it did not entirely constrain private initiative. While Dobbs' contemporaries shared his view that the able-bodied poor were the products of their own laziness and debauchery, they felt the need to offer some assistance to their impotent counterparts. Charity, moreover, was socially desirable for the preservation of harmony between rich and poor. In reference to the social control function of charity in Ireland during this period, Maxwell (1979: 135) has commented that 'it helped to keep the poor from dangerous rioting and that irreligious discontent which was bad for the country as a whole, for it threatened the foundations of a well-ordered society'. Charity, according to this view, was desirable because it promoted docility among the poor.

In the revolutionary political climate of the late eighteenth century, the viability of punishment as a means of controlling the able-bodied poor collapsed. Consequently, the distinction between the deserving impotent poor and undeserving able-bodied poor was undermined. This confronted the purveyors of charitable relief with new problems. In England and many other European countries, the relief of the poor had become the responsibility of the State. In Ireland, private charity was the only source of relief—occasionally religiously sponsored, but usually highly secular in character.

Scientific charity and public morality

The relief of the poor had moved towards the sphere of secular morality during the early modern era, which was concerned less with the transcendent and more with the preservation of public order and the promotion of the work ethic. While the process of secularisation was much less dramatic in Ireland than in England, where the Elizabethan reform represented a major social policy development, it was none the less significant (Brady, 1976: 47). The new *mentalité* involved a 'scientific' concept of charity aimed at controlling the distribution of charity (Woodroofe, 1962: 19). It was to shape crucially the nature of Irish social policy in the nineteenth century.

Mendicity societies developed in the early nineteenth century. Their *raison d'être* was to 'suppress' begging. The *First Report of the Dublin Mendicity Association* (1818: 10) proclaimed that the *main object* of the organisation was to prevent the necessitous poor, capable of labour, from procuring subsistence without useful industry. The decision to orient its activities towards the able-bodied poor was motivated by the growing problem of begging. As a Royal Commission chaired by Archbishop Whateley put it in the 1830s, with reference to Dublin, 'the doors of carriages and shops, to the interruption of business, were beset by crowds of unfortunate and clamorous beggars, exhibiting misery and decrepitude in a variety of forms and frequently carrying about in their persons and garments the seeds of contagious disease' (Whateley, 1836: 30).

The history of the Dublin Mendicity Association, founded in 1818, which has been described as 'a poor law in miniature', typifies the problems of charity organisations directed at the able-bodied poor, (Whateley Commission, 1836: 44). The strategy of the association had four basic elements, the first of which was to provide indoor relief for the mendicant poor in the association's asylum to those resident in Dublin for a period of at least six months. According to the Whateley Commission (1836: 30) this rule was 'not strictly adhered to'.

The association's premises were located in buildings belonging to the Dublin Society in Hawkins Street until 1826, when they moved to Moira House on Usher's Island (Starrat, 1832: 157–8). The Whateley Commission recorded that 'the relief which is given to the inmates of the asylum is food, together with a small pecuniary allowance to those incapable of work; to all others employment of such a nature as they may be thought capable of together with food, labour being enforced in all possible cases' (Whateley, 1836: 30).

Secondly, the Dublin Mendicity Association sought to impose settlement by returning the poor to their place of origin, whether it was in Ireland or Britain. Whateley (1836: 31) noted in reference to this stratagem:

> Amongst applications for relief at the asylum there are many who seek transmission home. Of the persons thus applying, all who are natives of Great Britain, if in great distress, and who, if able, are also willing to work, are sent to Liverpool without delay, with a small allowance for their support on the passage. Natives of the country parts of Ireland so applying, whether they be paupers reduced to extreme want in this city, are, upon like conditions, sent to such places as their relations or friends may reside in; but persons are not transmitted to England who have not settlements there.

Thirdly, the Dublin Mendicity Association sought to render mendicancy unprofitable. Whateley (1836: 31) observed: 'to this end, in all the annual reports which are published by the institutions, no opportunity is lost of discouraging indiscriminate alms-giving to the beggars in the streets; and carts are sent round the streets for the purpose of collecting broken victuals as otherwise would probably be given to beggars'. Fourthly, the Association sought to procure punishment for persistent beggars. It was singularly unsuccessful in achieving this goal due to a lack of co-operation from both the public and the courts.

The main features of 'scientific' charity (i.e. district committees, individual casework and record-keeping) were clearly visible in the rules of the Dublin Mendicity Association. These rules provided for a central directorate and a complicated committee structure which involved six sub-committees dealing with investigation, employment, supply, health, education, and superintendence as well as finance and accounts (*First Report of the Dublin Mendicity Association*, 1818: 12).

The Dublin Mendicity Association's rules were applied to individual cases through the medium of a system of district committees. Each

70

district committee was required to divide itself into a sub-committee structure equal in number and similar in name to those of the directorate. When a district had established this administrative machinery it was required to establish a 'patch' system:

> They shall then proceed to sub-divide their respective districts into walks, each so small in extent as to be completely within the scope of an individual's attention . . . Over each of these walks, they shall appoint one or more of their number as visitor. (*First Report of the Dublin Mendicity Association*, 1818: 15)

The visitors were empowered to give tickets to those deemed to be deserving of relief. The applicants were then required to present themselves to the district office, where members of the district sub-committee attended in rotation. The investigators compiled a profile of the applicants including details of age, residence, marital status, health, occupation and employability, dependants, previous aid from charitable sources, and character.

The acquisition of these details was followed by a thorough investigation of the application for assistance:

> When the applicants's answers to those queries have been entered into the schedule, he is to be dismissed for the present, and directed to return on a stated day; and the schedule is to be handed over to the visitor of the walk in which the applicant resides, who is to make inquiries at the place of residence, and in the neighbourhood, as to the truth of the answers; and having noted his remarks on the schedule, to return it to the office, with his opinion as to the mode of treatment to be adopted. These schedules are then to be laid before the District Sub-Committee of Investigation, who will determine on the treatment of the applicant, whether as to sustenance or work, of which he is to be apprised on the day named as above for his return; at which time, if a street-beggar, he is to be warned of the consequences of returning to his former mode of life. (*First Report of the Dublin Mendicity Association*, 1818: 17)

The fund-raising activities of the Dublin Mendicity Association demonstrate that the spirit of benevolence among the affluent towards the able-bodied poor remained tightly constrained. On occasion, less than scrupulous fund-raising methods were resorted to in order to stimulate their generosity. At a meeting of the Dublin Mendicity Association in 1819, its committee considered parading the beggars publicly. This course of action was rejected 'as inconsistent with those principles of industry, and unobtrusive decency of behaviour, which

71

your committee had so long and constantly endeavoured to inculcate' (Tenth Report of Dublin Mendicity Association, 1828: 9). However, by 1834 the lack of funds had become so critical that they had overcome their scruples about parading beggars, according to the English commentator, Henry Inglis (1835: 16–17) who admonishingly concluded: 'I cannot conceive anything more disgraceful to a civilised community'.

During the crisis year of 1826, when distress was particularly prevalent in Dublin, the *Freeman's Journal* (10 August) had produced a virtual obituary notice of the Mendicity Association, declaring that 'it is with sincere regret that we have learned that this most valuable institution is on the brink of dissolution'. This may have been one of the Mendicity Association's ploys to raise funds, since two years later it felt able to congratulate itself publicly on the achievements of its first decade:

> In coming before you to surrender their trust, and to account with you for the management of the Institution during the past year, your Committee cannot refrain from expressing, at the onset, their congratulations at the success which has so conspicuously attended the truly noble work undertaken by this Association. To have anticipated so happy a result must have been a hope which the most sanguine among the founders could scarcely have entertained; and were it possible that those who first conceived the project could have looked into futurity, and foreseen the many seasons of disease, misery, and distress with which it has pleased Providence to visit this City, their hearts might well have failed them in their first efforts, and the task might have been abandoned for ever. Famine and pestilence have appeared year after year; countless difficulties have been overcome, and it is now the just pride of this City that, under every discouragement, and against every obstacle, 'hoping against hope', a number of her Citizens have been found during all this period sufficient to supply the funds demanded for this great undertaking, and to furnish from among themselves those who have never shrunk from the care and labour of conducting its operations. (*Tenth Report of the Dublin Mendicity Association*, 1828: 9)

It cannot be doubted that the Dublin Mendicity Association did have large numbers of mendicants on its books, as was evident from the thousands recorded annually. However, it was superseded by the Poor Law of 1838 and Catholic charities as the primary voluntary force in the second half of the nineteenth century.

Catholicism, subsidiarity and assistencialism

The educational and caring role adopted by the Catholic Church highlights the metamorphosis that charity underwent in early modern society. Other than the charity sermon, intended to raise money for schools and orphanages, the Catholic Church was not significantly engaged in charitable enterprise in Ireland prior to the Great Famine. Keenan (1983: 25) has noted in this context that 'specifically Catholic charities can be traced back as far as 1750, though in a very small way'. Apart from fund-raising, the Catholic Church's charitable activities appear to have been largely oriented towards the moral needs of destitute children. In this regard, the *Catholic Directory* (1836: 166) observed 'in consequence of the limited means of Catholic charities many Catholic children have been thrown from time to time, by their parents, upon the bounty of Protestant and other schools adverse to the principles of Catholic religion'. It concluded that its mission was 'to restore children to the faith'. The moral care of the unmarried mother would likewise appear to have had evangelical purpose, given the references to female penitents and the application of the title Magdalene (i.e. reformed prostitute) to the homes that developed for the incarceration of this social group during the nineteenth century and the first half of the twentieth. Kerr (1982: 151) has reached a similar conclusion, arguing that the Government did not confer legitimacy on Roman Catholic charity until the Charitable Bequests Act, 1844, which 'was far more important than its provisions appeared to warrant'.

Catholic social philosophy came to be predicated on the concept of subsidiarity during the twentieth century, which was profoundly anti-statist. The concept of subsidiarity refers to a principle of Government endorsed by Pope Pius XI in the encyclical *Quadragesima Anno*, promulgated in 1931 which stated that:

> It is an injustice, a grave evil and a disturbance of right order, for a larger and higher association to arrogate to itself functions which can be performed efficiently by smaller and lower societies . . . Of its very nature, the true aim of all social activity should be to help the members of the social body, but never to destroy or absorb them . . . The State . . . should leave to smaller groups the settlement of business of minor importance, which otherwise would greatly distract it; it will carry out with greater freedom, power and success the tasks belonging to it alone . . . The more faithfully this principle of subsidiarity function be followed . . . the greater will be both social authority and social efficiency, and the happier and more prosperous the condition of the commonwealth. (*Quadragesima Anno*, 1931: paras 79–80).

Fr Jerome O'Leary (1954: 321), a prominent exponent of the doctrine of subsidiarity in Ireland, defined it in more simple terms. He wrote: 'a larger and higher association should not arrogate to itself functions which can be performed with reasonable efficiency by smaller and lower societies'. Fr O'Leary (1954: 320) also stated that 'if we accept, then, as we must, this principle of subsidiarity as being of universal validity, it follows that the State, like any other society, has a specific function of its own and is not entitled to take on any function which it pleases or any function which a misguided electorate may think fit to try to foist upon it'. The implications of the doctrine of subsidiarity for the social policy-makers in Ireland were abundantly clear. The State should not assume responsibility for social service provision if help could be alternatively provided through individual initiative, family assistance or voluntary association. As Fr O'Leary (1954: 61) put it, State 'intervention should always be regarded as merely a first-aid measure'.

In the Irish State, which was established in 1922, the principle of subsidiarity has become a dominant characteristic of social policy. However, the position of the Church as a social services provider had already been established, as noted above, following the Charitable Bequests Act, 1844. This law placed the Roman Catholic Church in a very powerful position within Irish society. It was given ownership and control of many of the schools, hospitals and social services in the country, power it continues to exercise to the present day. The Green Paper on the Community and Voluntary Sector (Department of Social Welfare, 1997: 31) acknowledges this powerful religious role:

> It is notable that the voluntary sector in Ireland not only complements and supplements State service provision, but is the dominant or sole provider in particular social services areas. In this context Roman Catholic religious organisations and those of other denominations have played a major role in the provision of services. Many services have been initiated and run by religious organisations, for example, services for people with a mental and physical disability, youth services, the elderly, residential child care services and services for the homeless.

The role of the Roman Catholic lay religious organisation, the St Vincent de Paul, which has 1,000 branches in Ireland and approximately 11,000 members, in providing welfare and various financial services has been acknowledged by the Green Paper (Department of Social Welfare, 1997: 31) as operating a 'shadow Welfare State'. This is an extraordinary admission in an official report. On the same page, the Green Paper makes its position clear by stating that 'the Government greatly values the vital role played by these various organisations and acknowledges the enormous contribution made by them in assisting individuals in need, the communities in which they live and work and society as a whole'. This statement is a powerful testament to the enduring power of the religious in Irish society and the role of the voluntary sector in maintaining that power. It also raises the problem of assistencialism. The Brazilian adult educator, Friere, criticised assistencialism for ignoring dialogue with the poor and imposing silence on them. He viewed it as an anti-democratic strategy. Moreover, as Regan recently noted, assistencialism prevents the poor 'from entering history as active critical agents of change' (*Irish Times*, 7 June 1997).

Given the numerous recent allegations of breaches of trust and abuse of power by the Roman Catholic clergy, notably in the residential child-care sector, the Government's ringing endorsement of its role would seem to be somewhat inappropriate. It also sits uneasily alongside the Green Paper's (Department of Social Welfare, 1997: 24) assertion that 'an active voluntary and community sector contributes to a democratic and pluralist society'. The Roman Catholic Church is not democratically accountable. This lack of accountability raises questions about a democratic deficit in a voluntary sector where it is probable, though this is not disclosed in the Green Paper, that the bulk of funding goes to the Roman Catholic Church. Furthermore, it is difficult to see how pluralism can be achieved within a denominationalist framework that is its very antithesis.

The Green Paper (Department of Social Welfare, 1997: 31) opines that 'the role of religious organisations in relation to the voluntary and community sector is changing', citing a decline in vocations and the 'withdrawal of religious personnel from some services'. The North Eastern Health Board (NEHB) region is used as an illustration of this purported change. The NEHB has recently had ownership of Our Lady of Lourdes Hospital, Drogheda, transferred to it. This development might be seen as symptomatic of a trend in which the religious surrenders institutional control to the State. However, that would be a simplistic analysis. The Green Paper (Department of Social Welfare, 1997: 31) notes that 'religious personnel have increased their role in, for example, community based services and are redressing their mission'.

75

In a study of voluntary organisations in the Eastern Health Board area (by far the largest in the country, including Dublin City in its boundaries), Faughnan and Kelleher (1993) found that 57% displayed multiple forms of religious involvement, which included religious being a founder member, providing significant finances, occupying the position of director and providing premises.

What appears to be happening is that religious involvement in the voluntary sector is mutating and evolving from its traditional ownership of the institutional voluntary sector to community participation, frequently in a leadership role. There is very little evidence of a decline in religious influence in a more secular society, rather there is evidence of a remarkable ability to adapt and to continue to exercise a hegemonic role. The underlying aspiration of the voluntary and community sector to promote democratic pluralism is fundamentally challenged by this on-going religious hegemony that remains the most durable influence in the Irish voluntary sector. It defies the long-term trend toward secularisation and secular values within Irish society as a whole. What is evident is that traditionalist influences continue to be highly influential in defining the concept of community in Ireland.

Communitarianism, emancipatory politics and cultural defenderism

Traditional accounts of the origins of communitarianism in Ireland and, more fundamentally, the ideological premise on which they rest, have tended to provide a very one-sided version of its history. Irish culture is rich in dichotomies. Perhaps there is no stronger dichotomy in the Irish world-view than the divide between traditional and modern cultural idioms. In the language of communitarianism, this tends to express itself in the cultural idyll of the traditional community with its iconography of pre-industrial forms as opposed to the technical alienating ethos of modern urban civilisation.

In sociological discourse this conceptual distinction has been famously made by the German social theorist, Ferdinand Tonnies, coining the almost untranslatable terms *Gemineshaft* and *Gessellschaft*. Tonnies, who is one of the most effective cultural pessimists among social theorists, described the state of *Gessellschaft* (society) in 1887 as one in which people were hostile to each other or bound together by mere contractual obligation. By contrast, *Gemineinschaft* (community) is founded on an essential sympathy and provides a 'natural' union of people in which force and the negative aspects of modern civilisation are

76

absent.

The confrontation of a wholesome community of minds in the past with the heartless contractual society of the present is historically misleading for two reasons. It is unlikely that a community of this kind ever existed; and it is certain that the reality that is idealised as communal was, in fact, much less agreeable than its glorification suggests. All human societies have social structures. There are always and everywhere those who are able to lay down the law and those, in a subordinate position, who are bound to obey. Probably for this reason, there has always been a struggle for greater equality, which rests at the heart of the logic of community development.

If the notion of 'community' were to refer to the traditional world of a more or less distant past, it should be stressed that the image of the rural idyll is quite incomplete without mentioning the poverty, sickness, famine, death and emigration that most accurately characterised pre-modern Ireland. This reality was to condition Irish social life until the modernisation project adopted in the 1960s. Modernisation redefined the meaning of community.

This leads back to the deconstruction of the idea of 'community' and its uses in a society that has taken the road to modernity with great hesitation. If one recognises that every society, including one's own, generates within it inequalities and struggles, one accepts by the same token the probability of change into an uncertain, or certainly open, different future. In this context, calling social inequalities and traditional ties by their names means questioning their legitimacy and making a beginning towards their transformation.

Ireland's road to modernity has been a long and troubled one. A persistent traditionalism of thought has weakened the effects of formal social citizenship rights, which have been gradually granted in law, politics and society; opportunities objectively granted have not been fully realised subjectively. Powerful social, cultural and political interests are deeply rooted in a traditionalist vision of Ireland, which have sought to hold the country in a State of semi modernity. They have been helped in their struggle against modernity by a selective history of communitarianism based on a struggle to preserve a traditionalist vision of Ireland. As a consequence, social citizenship rights have remained incomplete and chances for participation have continued, to the present day, to be more unequally distributed than the full status of citizenship in a modern democracy would permit. In this way, Irish society has made it difficult to articulate alternatives to the status quo that are fundamental to the practice of community development. Traditionalists continue to work hard to colonise the future through harnessing the ideal of community to their social and cultural objectives. Cosmic optimists, who see the liberating potential of modernity in terms of emancipatory and life politics, constantly seek to articulate an alternative vision. This alternative vision also has a historic basis in Irish society.

There are problems in assessing the nature of communitariansm in pre-modern Irish society as it was generally informal in character and, therefore, went unrecorded for posterity. None the less, there are references in the literature which indicate a culture of resistance in pre-modern Irish society. Mutual aid and utopian socialist initiatives in the field of co-operativisation suggest that there was an active alternative culture.

Mutual aid was part of the 'Alternative' Ireland which, as Foster has observed, 'has its own historiography and breeds its own controversies'. This subterranean culture is most brilliantly evoked in Daniel Corkery's celebrated study of the Munster poets, *The Hidden Ireland*. Corkery's book, published in 1924, extends well beyond its ostensible purpose, revealing a suppressed population of native Irish existing outside the bounds of colonial society with its own traditions and customs. While the iconography of the Munster poets celebrated Jacobite politics and recalled the lost world of the Gaelic aristocracy, a less patrician culture of resistance existed among the poor. It was dramatically associated with the social banditry of the Whiteboy movement. More prosaically, mutual aid evinced a spirit of cultural resistance. But in truth, like the political aspirations of the Gaelic aristocracy, mutual aid was an essentially romantic phenomenon which belonged to a doomed society.

Ireland during the nineteenth century witnessed the abrogation of the customary agrarian use rights of the common people. Their fate was either starvation and death from famine or, more likely, emigration to the New World or Britain to populate the burgeoning labour force that composed the army of capitalist enterprise. However, a culture of resistance continued and radical alternatives were espoused by utopian socialists such as William Thompson from Cork and Robert Owen, the architect of the New Lanark Community in Scotland. Owen revealed his *Plan for Ireland* in 1817, and subsequently presented it in modified form to the Select Committee on the Employment of the Poor in Ireland, 1823. Owen's *Plan for Ireland* was produced after some seven or eight months touring Munster, Leinster, and eastern Ulster. The *Plan*, inspired by his New Lanark experiment established in the 1790s, provided for co-operative village communities of 1,000 people renting or purchasing a farm of 1,000 acres, of medium-quality soil which would be subjected to spade cultivation. Owen went on to establish his New Harmony Community in Indiana, which was less successful. His ideas were not accepted by the Irish establishment, which he addressed.

Thompson, on the other hand, advocated his version of co-operation outside the established realms of power in Ireland. It led to the development of the Ralahine Community in the last years of his life, which became an internationally acknowledged success and was described as a 'mecca of social reforms'. Ralahine was destroyed by the unwillingness of the law to recognise common ownership rights. Its significance, none the less, was great. James Connolly (1956: 57) wrote:

> So Ralahine ended. But in the rejuvenated Ireland of the future the achievement of those simple peasants will be dwelt upon with admiration as a great and important landmark in the march of the human race towards its complete social emancipation.

It was a fulsome obituary. In reality the focus of emancipatory politics moved to the great social movements that emerged in the late nineteenth century and dominated early twentieth century politics. Most notable were the Labour Movement, led by James Connolly and James Larkin, and the Women's Movement, led by Hanna Sheehy Skeffington, Maud Gonne and others. Inevitably the struggle for nationhood and the politics of partition obscured wider issues of social emancipation, which received only token acknowledgement from Nationalists in the Democratic Programme, 1919. Resistance to the new Nationalist State soon emerged, giving birth to a vibrant atmosphere of social protest and community activism around core policy issues, notably unemployment and housing conditions.

In the slums, the Republican Congress was active during the 1930s in organising Tenants' Leagues which campaigned for rent reductions and against evictions. The Tenants' Leagues also helped to provide alternative accommodation. The organisation of the Tenants' Leagues led to the formation of the Property Owners' Association in autumn 1934. The *Irish Workers' Voice* described the formation of the Irish Property

Owners' Association as a 'crusade of cupidity', adding for good measure:

> The greedy, griping rapacious fingers of these harpies have plundered us for generations. But today, the workers cry 'Halt!' and fling in the face of this Property Owners' Association the demands of the Congress Tenants' Leagues. (*Irish Workers' Voice*, 3 November 1934)

The Irish Unemployed Workers' Movement also threw its active support behind the campaign against slum-landlordism, picketing the homes of those threatened with eviction. The organisation of Tenants' Leagues undoubtedly politicised the slum population, who were prepared to resist what they regarded as unfair impositions. For example, a rent strike was organised by the tenants of Liberty Flats in Dublin during the summer of 1939. During the wartime emergency demands were made for the stabilisation of rents at pre-War levels and the granting of a moratorium to the unemployed. The existence of a spirit of militancy among the poor and the role of the revolutionary Left in developing poor people's movements, such as the Tenants' Leagues, stands in marked contrast to the growing conservative influence of Catholic social thought in the theatre of Irish politics, notably on the issue of Constitutional reform which led to the highly regressive and deeply sectarian 1937 Constitution. The radical tradition of housing action was to resume in the post-War years, notably in the 1960s and 1970s.

The war-time emergency witnessed the suppression of social protest including the imprisonment of social activists, along with Republican prisoners. Radical newspapers were banned. Demonstrators were forcibly driven from the streets. The wartime emergency coincided with an increasingly conservative Fianna Fáil agenda that did not brook social or political protest.

Criticism of post-War Ireland's dismal economic performance was widespread, particularly in the Labour movement and among the unemployed. As the post-War world boomed during the 1950s, the Irish economy continued to founder. Restrictions on credit by banks were identified as being at the core of Ireland's lack of industrial development. Mass emigration returned to haunt the Irish population, questioning the legitimacy of the Irish nation state. Clearly, social change had to be embraced if the fledging Irish State was to retain the support and respect of its citizens. Modernisation proved to be the answer. However, several organisations, most notably Muintir na Tire, valiantly sought to defend the traditional, cultural values of rural Ireland against the forces of modernisation and industrialisation, which transformed rural Ireland and turned it into an urban society.

The influence of Muintir na Tire, founded by Father John Hayes in 1937, typifies the traditionalist element in the communitarian movement in Ireland. Forde (1996: 9) has underlined its cultural defenderist role, observing that, 'Muintir na Tire was established at a time when urbanisation was impinging on rural life, when communism was considered an international threat, and when the State began to play a more active role in social planning'. Muintir na Tire started as a co-operative but mutated into a system of parish councils. It was ideologically a deeply conservative movement. Forde (1996: 9) notes that 'Muintir na Tire refused to acknowledge the possibility of class or other conflict in its parish councils, which are organised on a vocational basis with representation from all the main class groupings in the parish'.

In 1958, Muintir na Tire adopted the UN definition of community development that emphasised partnership between the State and local communities (Forde, 1996: 9). Following the Irish modernisation project, initiated in the 1960s, the pace of rural decline was sharply increased, weakening Muintir na Tire. In order to combat this decline Muintir na Tire embarked on a programme of reorganisation in the 1970s, and parish councils were replaced by democratically elected community councils. Forde (1996: 10) has assessed the strengths and weaknesses of community councils as follows:

> It could be argued that the strengths of community councils lie in their ability to provide local amenities, such as community centres, in the organisation of leisure activities, and in lobbying the State for improvements in local facilities. Their weaknesses include their failure to develop sufficiently to offer employment to professional workers, their inactivity for large periods of the year and their inadequacies in planning and managerial terms.

The decline in the role of Muintir na Tire continued. The number of parish councils fell from 300 in the 1970s to 120 in 1990 (Forde, 1996: 10).

This decline was primarily due to the onward march of rural decay. However, there has been a concomitant shift in the direction of community development. As Crickley and Devlin (1990: 54) have noted, 'during the last decade, community work shifted its emphasis from an overall concern with issues in a geographical area to a focus on specific interests and communities of interest e.g. training, employment, women, youth, Traveller and minority groups'. However, the cultural defenderist ethos that Muintir na Tire represents is far from dead. The American Sociologist, Amitai Etzioni, in his influential book entitled *The Spirit of Community*, shares this outlook. Etzioni (1994: 2) defines what he calls the communitarian thesis as an attempt 'to shore up our values, responsibilities and communities'.

The problem with the cultural defenderist vision of community is that it is anti-modernist. In Ireland its roots in cultural defenderism have militated against a socially progressive response to modernisation. In a world where the politics of recognition have become dominant (e.g. the Women's movement, the Ecological movement, the Black Power movement, the Gay Rights movement), organisations such as Muintir na Tire have become increasingly marginalised. Single issues campaigns in recent years, like the fishing rod licence dispute, have served to marginalise further traditional organisations like Muintir na Tire in rural Ireland.

The new politics of postmodernity

The Green Paper on the Community and Voluntary Sector (Department of Social Welfare, 1997: ii) sets out, as already noted, 'to suggest a framework for the future development of the relationship between the State and community and the voluntary sector and to facilitate a debate on the issues relevant to their relationship'. This project would appear to be set to forge a new social language for Ireland. At the heart of this task is the redefinition of 'community' in postmodern society. The Welfare State, the great project of the post-War era, sought to define community in terms of social citizenship. The 1980s changed the emphasis to the duties and obligations of citizenship. It is a notable feature of the 1990s that in the United States, the Clinton Administration has declared its opposition to welfare dependency. Government in Ireland would appear to have inexorably moved in the same direction, albeit in a less divisive way because of the influence of the ideal of the European social market economy. In Britain the 'New Labour' Administration, elected in 1997, intends to replace the Beveridgian Welfare State, and seeks to end welfare dependency. Society seems to be moving beyond the traditional post-War collectivist conception of citizenship as membership of the Welfare State to embracing a form of progressive individualism in a community context. On the face of it, the parallels with the acquisitive individualism of the 1980s are unmistakable, suggesting that the latter may still be setting the agenda. However, the individualism of the Nineties lacks the cultural narcissism of the 1980s and seeks to harness the liberating potential of life politics to its more traditionally emancipatory political concerns and, perhaps most significantly, to replace the State by the community as the primary social institution through an inclusive politics of partnership. It would seem that we have reached the outer limits of the State's capability to organise society. Community has once again come of age, albeit in a new form—a partnership typified by the philosophy of the Green Paper (Department of Social Welfare, 1997) on the Community and Voluntary Sector in Ireland and its relationship with the State.

In order to demonstrate the nature of this change, it is necessary to analyse the meaning of citizenship within postmodern society by identifying the major economic, political, social and cultural changes we are experiencing, its relationship to the new project of the 1990s and, particularly, the implications for community development.

On the economic front, postmodern society is characterised by the decline in the capacity of the nation state for effective economic intervention and its replacement by global economic blocks (e.g. the European Union/NAFTA). The task of Government has consequently moved in a significant way to Brussels. For example, the Social Chapter provides a framework for employment conditions throughout Europe. However, the Social Chapter needs to be set in the context of deindustrialisation and deregulation, which are undermining traditional workers' rights forged through struggle during the twentieth century. With the rise of the East Asian economies, characterised by low wages and authoritarian States, the bargaining position and employability of workers in traditional industries have been undercut. Increasingly, local communities shattered by economic dislocation are being asked to to unemployment in the 1990s.

On the political front, the problems of redefining citizenship in postmodern society are complex. The traditional working-class solidarity on which the Welfare State was constructed has collapsed in postmodern society. There is now in Ireland a one-third/two-thirds society, as noted in Chapter 3. This is part of a global phenomenon, as already stated, known as 'the Brazilianisation of the West'. The one-third form an underclass effectively excluded from participation in both the labour market and the political process, which they do not perceive as relevant

83

to their needs. The exclusion of the underclass from meaningful participation in citizenship and the alienation in general of the youth population in the inner cities are among the most pressing problems that the country faces. Security has become a key political issue as the majority seek to protect themselves form the social consequences of sharpening inequalities, notably crime, drugs and violence. Society arguably needs to rediscover the idiom which acknowledges the citizenship rights of this alienated minority. This will require (a) the broadening of political debate beyond a preoccupation with narrow economic concerns; (b) the creation of participatory democratic institutions at grass-roots community level; and (c) information which empowers the citizen to know and understand what is going on in an increasingly changing society. The Green Paper on the Community and Voluntary Sector (Department of Social Welfare, 1997: 24) recognises the need for 'a more participatory democracy where active citizenship is fostered'. Active citizenship is fundamental to its vision of postmodern Ireland. The Green Paper commits itself to fostering civil society.

On the social and cultural front, the dominant themes of postmodernity are community and family. This is no accident. As the limitations of the State have become increasingly visible since the mid-1970s, it was perhaps inevitable that people would turn to re-embedding more traditional institutions for security. However, there is a danger that this turning back to traditional institutions will be frustrated by a misreading of the processes of social change, since the community and the family are also being fundamentally reshaped in postmodern society. This is the paradox of our times!

Those who grasp this process of change sometimes tend to come to profoundly pessimistic conclusions about the state of our culture. A frequently painted picture is of erosion of social ties, the weakening of civil society and, at its most extreme, the break-up of society. This analysis is also based on a complete misreading of cultural trends. There are, of course, as already adverted to, disturbing phenomena in postmodern society, notably the growth in crime and anti-social behaviour. It is also true that some institutions are in decline: the traditional nuclear and extended family, and some traditional large social organisations, such as political parties, the Churches and the rural associations. It would be utterly wrong, however, to infer from this that civil society is in decline in Ireland.

84

On the contrary, one of the great trends of the past 30 years during which Ireland has modernised has been exactly the opposite: civil society, far from weakening, has grown richer and denser. What is true is that civil society, in becoming more diverse, has grown more fragmented. The danger with the ideal of community is that it is determinedly backward-looking. The term itself immediately evokes a picture of locality.

The problem, therefore, with the traditionalist's notion of voluntarism and community is that it would appear to value only the local community. It does not recognise that the weakening of locality has been accompanied by the emergence of many other forms of voluntary and community action and collectivity, based on interest, gender, ethnicity, hobby, friendship, profession or knowledge, and these virtual collectivities may be local, regional, national, European or even global— think of the Internet. In other words, the growing diversity and complexity of civil society describes the emergence of the many more identities now available to us, all of which by definition are social in nature.

Consequently, the traditionalists' championship of community represents a form of cultural essentialism or fundamentalism. Its rejection of modernity consigns it to oblivion in postmodern society because of its limited purchase on the present and incapacity to comprehend or address the future. It represents an emotion rather than a guide. It is clear that, if community is to become a core institution in a society from which it has been disembedded, it must re-embed itself in new forms that connect with the realities and possibilities of a greatly developed civil society in the 1990s.

Where do voluntary action and community development fit into the structures of postmodern society? We have noted the changing nature of the postmodern project in the West. It is, however, impossible to ignore the momentous events of 1989, when the Communist world collapsed. This raises challenging questions about the future. Will the historical symbiosis between capitalism and democracy that characterised the West be generalised on a global scale? Should we not see the return to nationalism, fascism and racism in Europe precisely as a reaction to this process of global unification? What future has community development as a vehicle for social action and change in this new social order?

One can take the pessimistic view and envisage the future role of voluntary and community activists in terms of defensive politics as Governments increasingly temporise with racists, cut wages and unleash the full forces of the unbridled market. As social divisions widen between class groups, gender groups and ethnic groups, community activists can seek to advocate the cause of social justice by helping the socially excluded to challenge fundamental inequalities. The politics of participation can become the touchstone of voluntary action and community development in the twenty-first century as the emancipatory political dreams of the twentieth century disappear into the realms of historical curiosity. That is the pessimistic scenario. It suggests a vital but Sisyphean role for community development in the future.

On the other hand, one can embrace a more cosmically optimistic view of the future of the world and the role of voluntarism and community development. The political changes we are witnessing at the end of this century are undoubtedly profound. But, arguably, even more profound changes are taking place in which the modernity with which we are familiar is being replaced by a new modernity, which some sociologists call postmodernity, others high-modernity, yet others post-industrial society or the information society. They agree, however, that this is a 'reflexive modernity' which is qualitatively different to anything experienced by humankind to date.

Reflexive modernity is variously defined by sociologists. The distinguished Cambridge sociologist, Tony Giddens (1991: 20) states that:

> Modernity's reflexivity refers to the susceptibility of most aspects of social activity, and material relations with nature, to chronic revision in the light of new information or knowledge. Such information or knowledge is not incidental to modern institutions, but constitutive of them - a complicated phenomena, because many possibilities of reflections about reflexivity exist in modern social conditions.

Beck *et al.* (1994: 6) commenting from a German perspective, have declared that 'reflexive modernisation means self-confrontation with the effects of risk society that cannot be dealt with and assimilated in the system of industrial society—as measured by the latter's institutionalised standards'.

If the analyses of these social theorists of postmodernity is correct, we are entering a new era with greater potential for change than ever envisaged before. The nature of this change ironically defies control, suggesting boundless potentialities for reframing the core social issues.

The argument of Beck *et al.* that social confrontation is seminal to the process of reflexive modernity is illustrative.

Beck *et al.* contend that postmodern society (or risk society, as they term it) 'is by tendency also a self-critical society'. We are all aware that we live in an era of radical doubt. There are no longer taboos or sacred cows. In this society, self-criticism abounds. As Beck *et al.* (1994: 11) put it:

> Insurance experts (involuntarily) contradict safety engineers. While the latter diagnose zero risk, the former decide uninsurable. Experts are undercut or deposed by opposing experts. Politicians encounter the resistance of citizens' groups, and industrial management encounters morally and politically motivated organised consumer boycotts. Administrations are criticised by self-help groups. Ultimately, even polluter sectors (for instance, the chemical industry in the case of sea pollution) must count upon resistance from affected sectors (in this case the fishing industry and sectors living from seashore tourism). The latter can be called into question by the former, monitored and perhaps even corrected. Indeed, the risk issue splits families, occupational groups from skilled chemical workers all the way up to management, often enough even individuals themselves. What the head wants and the tongue says might not be what the hand (eventually) does.

Beck *et al.* (1994: 11) conclude that the multiple antagonisms, despite their diffuse and ambivalent natures, are 'hollowing out the political co-ordinates of the old industrial society'. Recently, Beck (1997: 98) has argued that we are reinventing politics, 'in short a double world is coming into existence one part of which cannot be depicted by the other: a world of symbolically rich political institutions and a world of often concealed political practices (conflicts, power games, instruments and arenas)'.

Conclusion

Arguably, this cosmic optimism is warranted. The Cold War era was characterised by a petrification of criticism. The ideological glue that held society together, East and West, throughout the twentieth century has dissolved. As noted above, in postmodern society, traditional class structures, family patterns and belief systems are all breaking down. However, this does not, as cultural pessimists suggest, leave a vacuum with nothing tangible to take the place of traditional forms. New forms are emerging. Emancipatory politics are being complemented by life politics. The Women's Movement, and Gay and Lesbian Movement and the Ecological Movement are indicative of the intersection of the traditional politics of change with the new politics of the community, which adds lifestyles and existential security issues to the political agenda. Social movements and protest groups have become the vehicles of social and political action. While the traditional notions of voluntarism and community development based on locality have become redundant through the disembedding of traditional communities, new possibilities exist for re-embedding through the new structures of post-industrial society and the new technologies which have transformed communication. The role of community development in colonising the future must be pivotal. In a world characterised by constant confrontation and self-criticism, voluntarism and community development cannot but prosper as a vehicle for alternative political action if they adapt to the new forms of discourse. There can be little doubt that the twenty-first century promises to be more challenging for community developers, who have an unprecedented opportunity to colonise the future.

Chapter 5: Deconstructing Voluntarism in a Partnership Society

As identified and discussed in previous chapters, the intellectual concepts of active citizenship and the promotion of civil society are closely aligned with a resurgence of interest in voluntarism and a reliance on the voluntary sector in many areas of social life. For the advocates of welfare pluralism, the expression of active citizenship, community empowerment and local democracy are clearly based on the existence of a vibrant voluntary sector. Advocates of communitarianism, such as Etzioni, view volunteering as being essential to the expression of civil commitment (Etzioni, 1994: 261). Volunteering as a form of civil commitment is closely related to the existence of a dense network of voluntary organisations that create and sustain a healthy civic society.

The discussion of the relationship between citizenship and the voluntary sector is only one component of the discussion of citizenship in relation to the overall mixed economy of welfare – voluntary, statutory, commercial and community sectors of social provision. From this perspective, the challenges to the Welfare State posed by the partnership model have major implications for the contribution of the voluntary and community sector to the definition of citizenship in a postmodern era. This exchange of ideas, values and language is captured in the Green Paper on the Community and Voluntary Sector (Department of Social Welfare, 1997: 26) which asserts that 'the promotion and strengthening of social dialogue across society involves the State developing partnerships with a wide range of institutions, including not only the voluntary and community sector but also employed and trade unions'. This model is illustrated in Fig. 5.1.

The Green Paper (Department of Social Welfare, 1997: 22) sets out the challenges to postmodern Irish society:

> The existence of a differentiated society whereby a significant proportion of people are marginalised is incompatible with active and equal citizenship. The result for the marginalised is passivity, apathy, indifference and demoralisation. The consequence is a divided society that creates a dependent

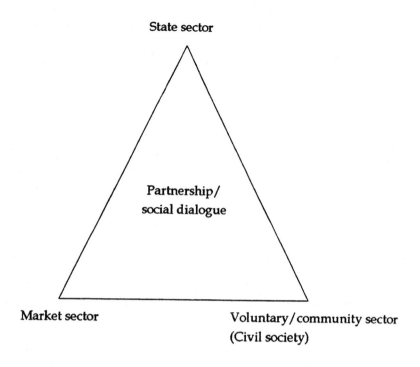

State sector

Partnership/
social dialogue

Market sector

Voluntary/community sector
(Civil society)

Fig. 5.1 The Social Partnership Model

class which is alienated, voiceless and has little stake in society. The cohesion of society and consequently its stability are at risk if people are unable to participate fully in the economic and social development of that society.

The Green Paper also offers a solution:

Although the solution envisaged is not a centralised solution, it presupposes the central allocation of resources within a facilitative and enabling framework which promotes what is known as 'civil society'. It requires the development of an enabling and open State which is engaged in dialogue and partnership and which allows bottom-up responses to emerge from voluntary organisations and community groups . . . It requires a philosophy reflecting what is sometimes called an 'enabling State' or 'assisted self reliance'.

The Green Paper is imaginative in its strategy. What is apparent is that the concept of voluntarism has been recontextualised in postmodern society within the language and ideology of communitarianism. Within this vision a symbiotic relationship is envisaged between the community/voluntary sector and the State. It is engineered through the concept of partnership, advocated as the strategy for the future. Philosophically, this is a powerful theme for the development of the voluntary sector. It envisages nothing less than an 'enabling State' based on a social market economy positioned in the overall framework of the European Union. But the essence of the partnership model for the Welfare State can be elusive. Precious little analytic work has been done on the connections of the Irish voluntary sector with a democratic communitarian vision of Irish society. This consideration is the focus for the rest of the study.

The core question is therefore the definition of the distinctive contribution of the voluntary/community sector in terms of the nature of voluntarism, the values of the sector and their relationship to civic trust, the structure of the voluntary sector, the changing focus of voluntary organisations and their distinctive contributions. The analysis will also draw on the research findings of the UCC Social Studies Research Unit. A full tabular presentation of the findings of the research is presented in this chapter and Appendix 5.

Defining voluntarism and the values of the sector

Defining voluntarism is largely concerned with placing conceptual parameters on the provision of unpaid service by volunteers in a structured organisational setting. At a practical level, voluntarism, according to Gladstone (1979: 26), involves a group of individuals who freely associate without a commercial motive to further their own welfare or the welfare of others. Voluntarism is also a function of moral principles, which imply duties to give to others. Spicer (1988), drawing on the work of Feinberg (1980), outlines several of these principles. They include: (1) indebtedness, where one person owes something to another; (2) reparation, where one person has to compensate another for harm done, and (3) duties owed within families or according to status. Finally, Spicer (1988: 31) argues that there are also a number of other duties which are general or 'humanitarian' because they are owed to everyone (like giving to charity or the duty to meet people's basic needs). The evolution of the Welfare State has in fact, according to De Swann (1988: 113), been a civilising process where there has been a gradual development towards statutory arrangements to deal with the basic welfare needs of the mass of the population.

A significant strand in the social construction of voluntarism has been largely based on identifying the psychological basis for pro-social behaviour. One response has been that altruism is instinctive or inborn (Spicer, 1988: 33). This has been challenged on the basis that while it may explain why individuals help those that they are close to, such as parents or children, it does not explain why strangers are helped—which is the classic definition of altruistic behaviour. Another argument for the explanation of volunteering is founded on theories of social exchange and reciprocal benefit (i.e. the nature of volunteering as a social act from which volunteers derive benefits such as enjoyment of co-workers' company, conviviality and the sharing of experiences (Pearce, 1993: 78). However, according to Gerard (1985: 16), this is not the full story—discussion of motives needs to be broadened to include, at the very least, *beneficience* and *solidarity*.

For Gerard (1985: 16), beneficence calls on people to help others not on the basis of expected returns, but from 'a personal view which stresses notions of hierarchy, personal duty and compassion'. Looney (1986: 135) has argued that traditional voluntarism accords well with elements of traditional conservatism—the reduction in State-provided welfare services and the importance of individual initiative. However, not all supporters of the New Right are entirely happy with the growing interrelationship between the State and the voluntary sector. Looney (1986: 137) writes that for some advocates of the New Right, the voluntary sector is getting too much money, compassion has become professionalised and indignation provides a livelihood.

Solidarity, as described by Gerard (1985) and Bulmer (1986), in contrast, entails notions of fraternity and identity with the deprived. It is associated frequently with a commitment to political and social change. There is also a strong emphasis on the elimination of difference between helper and helped. The clearest elimination of this distinction is within the self-help organisations. This emphasis on solidaristic impulses has been at the root of many of the new voluntary organisations, which have emerged throughout all countries with developed Welfare States since the 1960s. These solidaristic impulses have revealed themselves in relation to organisational changes, which occurred within voluntary organisations (i.e. the trend towards greater 'bottom-up' involvement and community engagement), as well as within different orientations towards statutory interventions.

The UCC survey of the general population, as indicated in chapter 1, indicates a greater willingness among the volunteer population to look to the voluntary sector as the main provider of social care. In Table 5.1, it is shown that just over a third of the total population (35%) support the proposition that it is better for voluntary organisations to look after vulnerable members of society than for the State to look after them. This finding contrasts with the stronger level of support indicated by the volunteer section of the population, of whom 39% are in favour of voluntary organisations looking after vulnerable members of society rather than the State.

Table 5.1. Percentage of population who believe that it is better for voluntary organisations rather than the State to look after vulnerable members of society

	% of general pop.	% of pop. who have had involvement with voluntary organisations	% of pop. who have had no involvement with voluntary organisations
agree	35	39	31
disagree	55	50	46

The evidence from the UCC survey would also suggest that there is support for the conclusion that involvement with a voluntary organisation is not negatively associated with a belief in public expenditure on statutory services (see Table 1, Appendix 5). Overall, 42% of the population would favour increased taxation to fund increased public expenditure on welfare services, to be distributed through statutory mechanisms rather than through voluntary organisations. Interestingly, 47% of the volunteer section of the population agreed with this proposition, as compared with 38% of the non-volunteer section of the population.

In Table 5.2 there is some evidence that respondents who are involved with voluntary organisations are more in favour of the building of social networks through community involvement. Although the figures just fail to reach statistical significance, a remarkable 78% of respondents who had involvement with voluntary organisations would like to be more involved with people in their local community, compared with 71% of the population as a whole. The volunteer population demonstrate a higher rate of positive appreciation of the value of community involvement. These findings bear out the widely held belief that the volunteer section of a population adheres more strongly to values such as altruism, awareness of community and a sense of civic responsibility than the wider population as a whole.

Table 5.2. Percentage of population who would like the people in the local community where they live to be more involved with each other

	% of general pop.	% of pop. who have had involvement with voluntary organisations	% of pop. who have had no involvement with voluntary organisations
agree	71	78	67
disagree	17	15	18

The positive correlation between voluntarism and community involvement demonstrates, to some extent, a degree of identification with Fukuyama's concept of 'trust'. The volunteer component of the population would appear to have a higher acceptance of the norms of civic responsibility and social obligation. Citizens' involvement in non-familial organisations marked by high degrees of co-operation and non-bureaucratic structures, according to Fukuyama (1995), is a positive indicator of their level of trust in society. It also corresponds closely to Putnam's (1995) discussion of an active community involving notions of civic virtue, community and obligations of citizenship. Again, these findings support the proposition that volunteers are less oriented towards possessive individualism. At one level this finding would support other research results, which found that employees in the voluntary sector are less cynical and gain more satisfaction than their counterparts in the private and Government sectors (Kendall and Knapp, 1995: 72). On the other hand, studies of motivations of volunteers for joining have equally stressed what Pearce has termed the self-oriented aspects of volunteering such as career advancement and social networking (Pearce, 1993: 63).

The national opinion survey also indicated that volunteers tend to be more opposed to the egoism and selfishness of consumerism and market values than the population as a whole (Table 5.3). The extent to which individuals believe that to survive in life you must grab what you can and not worry about other members of society is significantly related to whether or not they have had involvement with voluntary organisations. More than three-quarters (76%) of the volunteer population opposed self-aggrandisement and the abandonment of social obligation compared, with two-thirds (66%) of the population as a whole. These findings suggest that volunteers are basically altruistic rather than self-interested people.

Table 5.3. Percentage of population who believe that to survive in this life you must grab what you can and not worry about other members of society too much

	% of general pop.	% of pop. who have had involvement with voluntary organisations	% of pop. who have had no involvement with voluntary organisations
agree	26	20	30
disagree	66	76	61

The volunteer section of the population also believes more strongly in the homogeneous nature of Irish society. In Table 5.4, it is shown that there is a marginally stronger belief (though not statistically significant) among the volunteer section of the population in the homogeneity of the value system of the Irish population (65%) as compared to 62% of the population who have had no involvement with the voluntary sector. The presence of shared ethical values is a vital component of what Fukuyuma (1995: 40) calls 'shared ethical habits', which are a key element in the maintenance of a healthy civil society.

On the axis of liberal vs. conservative, the results of the national opinion survey as presented in Table 2 (Appendix 5) show that 40% of the population believe that Ireland has become too liberal and wish to return to the way things were in the past. The remaining sections of the population were approximately evenly divided: 31% believed that Ireland had reached the right balance in its attitudes towards issues such as divorce, single parents, abortion and homosexuality and 27% believed that Ireland needed to become more liberal.

Table 5.4. Percentage of population who believe that Ireland is still a fairly united society because most people hold the same values when it comes to important matters

	% of general pop.	% of pop. who have had involvement with voluntary organisations	% of pop. who have had no involvement with voluntary organisations
agree	64	65	62
disagree	23	27	20

Anheier and Salamon (1994: 1), who have carried out some of the most comprehensive comparative research on the voluntary sector in a number of countries, have concluded that the size and visibility of the non-profit sector and the level and breadth of private charitable giving are far from crucial signs of the presence of a 'caring tradition' in a society. They go on to argue that the non-profit sector is only one possible embodiment of a society's caring tradition, and by no means necessarily the most significant one. Depending on the national circumstances, the State or business enterprises have assumed major caring responsibilities. Indeed, reliance on a strong voluntary sector may actually signify the absence, or weakness, of a caring tradition elsewhere in society or the resistance to alternative expressions of caring (Anheier and Salamon, 1994: 1). Kramer *et al.* (1993: 7) have argued that the research literature on voluntary organisations can be divided into two main types: the first type of study is concerned with *why* there are third-sector organisations and *what* accounts for the variations in the size and scope of the sector in different countries. The second type of study is devoted to *how* they are different from statutory and commercial organisations in their structure, governance and effectiveness.

Despite the acceptance of the considerable international diversity in both inherent values and organisational contribution to social services, common conceptions remain as to the values attached to the voluntary sector. Marshall (1996: 48–51) provides a useful summary of some of these conceptions. In each case the reality is far more complex than what these common conceptions imply.

1. Voluntary organisations are about volunteering.
2. The voluntary sector is more personalised, closer to the community: the statutory sector is bureaucratic.
3. The statutory sector serves consensus values: the minority sector is able to respond to minority values.
4. The voluntary sector is primarily concerned with the disadvantaged.
5. Control in the voluntary sector lies with the community, not with investors (private sector) or the Government (statutory).
6. The voluntary sector is creative, innovative, flexible and quick to respond.

Evidence from intensive interviews carried out with selected voluntary organisations in the Cork and Dublin regions suggests that the positive conceptions of the sector, suggested by Marshall, are strongly incorporated into organisational identity (see Appendix 1 for a full list of the organisations interviewed). In particular, practically all respondents believed that the voluntary sector is capable of being much more innovative than its statutory counterparts.

Typical views elicited from the respondents were that:

> *The voluntary sector provides a service for which there is no statutory equivalent.* (respondent from an organisation providing information and mediation services)

> *The voluntary sector have always been to the fore in developing new services. They are not subject to the same regulatory requirements as the State bodies.* (respondent from an organisation providing services to physically disabled people)

Another positive dimension stressed by respondents, is the capacity of the voluntary sector to offer a unique opportunity for members of the public to participate in civic-minded activities. All the respondents believed that the voluntary sector offered special qualities or enhanced citizenship that could not be replicated by increased public expenditure on statutory services. Seven respondents (16 interviews took place) made special reference to the encouragement of civic values among the population by introducing young people to voluntary work as part of the school curriculum.

Institutions of the sector

The opportunities for civic participation and the location of unique organisational values are expressed within a highly diverse voluntary sector. O'Donovan and Varley (1995: 3) emphasise the degree of research energy that has been invested in developing classificatory schemes and typologies of voluntary agencies. It is possible to identify typologies based on organisational culture (Handy, 1988), extent of relationships with the State (Cousins, 1978) and primary purpose of the voluntary agency (Smith *et al*, 1988; O'Donovan and Varley, 1996: 3). A broader interpretative typology for defining the institutional basis of the voluntary sector has been proposed in the UK *Report of the Commission on the Future of the Voluntary Sector* (1996: 20). This typology is based on the international study conducted from Johns Hopkins University (USA), which identified a *broad* and a *narrow* voluntary sector. The broad sector includes those organisations that are formally constituted, independent of Government and self-governing, not directly run by a for-profit agency or the State and not distributing any profits or delivering financial services. The narrow sector excludes organisations that are insufficiently altruistic.

The UK Royal Commission definition would exclude sports and social clubs, higher education, and trade union and business associations. This distinction, premised on the degree of altruism associated with an organisation's activities, also captures difficulties with the Irish legal definition of voluntary organisation. There is no official register of charities in Ireland. In order to be recognised as having charitable status for the purposes of the tax code, the objects of an organisation must be *entirely charitable* and charitable has a specific meaning for these purposes, i.e.

- the relief of poverty
- the advancement of religion
- the advancement of education
- other purposes of a charitable nature beneficial to the community (Cousins, 1994: 7).

This definition confers charitable status on many voluntary hospitals, secondary schools and sports clubs, which need not necessarily have *philanthropic* (actions performed by people who are not themselves in need for those who are) or *mutual aid* (people in need helping each other and in the process helping themselves) purposes.

Knight (1993) has elaborated on this definitional complexity. He has transformed it into six main categories of voluntary organisation, ranging from 'service philanthropy' at one end of the spectrum to community-based groups concerned chiefly with self-expression at the other extreme (see Table 5.6). Somewhat apart from the rest are intermediary or 'umbrella' bodies, which are concerned with developing the sector itself through providing advice and services to members (Knight: 1993). There is therefore considerable diversity and complexity, making it difficult to arrive at a precise definition of what the voluntary sector constitutes and means in contemporary society.

Table 5.6. Categories of voluntary organisation

Service philanthropy: The dominant forms of voluntary action, the helper is some social distance from the helped	Intermediaries: These have bureaucratic functions of development, provision of service to other organisations, liaison, and representation	Mobilising: The purpose is to locate money or volunteers for causes
Social Solidarity: The helper is part of the target group being helped	Change: The object is to change the behaviour or attitude of others	Creating: The purpose is to express self in the company of others.

(Source: Knight, 1993)

The UCC national survey of voluntary organisations reveals a distinct tendency by many organisations to move from a service philanthropic role to one based on social solidarity. The evidence from the research also supports the view that there have been considerable organisational changes along the remaining parameters provided by Knight's typology.

Contacted organisations were based on the complete list of organisations listed in the NSSB directory of social service organisations. Of the 579 organisations listed, 223 responded with completed questionnaires (see Appendix 1 for a description of the methodology underpinning the empirical research). The categorisation scheme used has similarities to that used by O'Mahony in her study of the voluntary sector in Co. Mayo in 1980 (O'Mahony, 1981: 160). That classification scheme was also largely oriented on the local vs. national dimension of an organisation's activities.

In Table 5.7, it will be noted that the largest proportion of respondents (46%) identified themselves as having a national co-ordination function with affiliated branches. The high level of responses in this category can be explained by reference to the type of organisation listed in the NSSB directory, many of which supply services on a nationwide basis.

Table 5.7. Type of organisation based on results of survey

Type of organisation	N	%
National voluntary organisation operating from one centre/branch	64	28%
Local voluntary group (Dublin) operating from one centre/branch	11	5%
Local voluntary group (not Dublin) operating from one centre/branch	14	6%
National voluntary organisation with affiliated branches/groups/etc.	102	46%
Local voluntary organisation (Dublin) with affiliated branches	5	2%
Local voluntary organisation (not Dublin) with affiliated branches	4	2%
National voluntary organisation working with non-affiliated groups	12	5%
Local voluntary organisation (Dublin) working with non-affiliated groups	3	1%
Local voluntary organisation (not Dublin) working with non-affiliated groups	1	0.4%
Other	7	3%

Valid cases 222   Missing cases 1

The UCC research has found that 60% of organisations were formed since 1971, with 34% of organisations formed since 1981 (Table 5.8). These results reinforce the previous findings: Ruddle and Donoghue's (1995: 26) study of Irish voluntary organisations in the social welfare area found that the average age of selected organisations was 17 years (*circa* 1978).

100

Table 5.8. When organisations were formed

Range of years	N	% of valid cases
Before 1900	11	5%
1901–10	1	0.5%
1911–20	1	0.5%
1921–30	3	1%
1931–40	8	4%
1941–50	7	3%
1951–60	9	4%
1961–70	30	14%
1971–80	57	26%
1981–90	73	34%
1991–96	15	7%

Valid cases 215   Missing cases 8

The findings of the UCC research and of Ruddle and Donoghue's work support Jaffro's (1996: 2) view that the 1970s was a crucial period when a new wave of community-based organisations came to life with a view to supporting and promoting citizen participation and activism in the community. They also provide clear evidence that, contrary to the popular view, modernity has not wiped out civil society. Landry and Mulgan have argued that the rise of associations, has been one of the most distinctive features of the postmodern world (Landry and Mulgan, 1995: 64). They refer to an 1982 study carried out by Salamon, which concluded that 65% of the organisations in 16 US communities had been created since 1960, particularly movements based on civil rights, feminism, environmentalism and conservative moralism, as evidence to support their argument. The 1970s have also been described as a 'critical decade in the evolution of statutory social services in Ireland' (Faughnan, 1990: 28). The expansion of statutory and voluntary services in the 1960s and 1970s was a response by Irish society to the complexities of the demand for modern social services. A central feature of these changes was the modernisation of social services, primarily through the provision of services in the community. This response, across a number of sectors (most clearly identified in the Commission of Inquiry into Mental Handicap, 1965 and the Report on the Care of the Aged, 1966) placed significant emphasis on funding voluntary organisations to supply services in the community. Curry (1980: 189) has observed in this regard that:

> The basic social services, housing, education, health and income maintenance cater for needs, which are common to all groups in society. However certain groups have special needs, and services over and above the basic services have evolved to cater for these needs. Such groups include the elderly, deprived children and the handicapped (both physical and mental). While these groups are catered for to some extent by the basic services, special provision is also required . . . It is in the field of welfare services that voluntary effort plays its greatest role.

The evidence, based on the UCC survey of voluntary organisations, is of an evolving service characterised by change and complexity. Tables 5.9 and 5.10 demonstrate the degree of difference between the past and present roles of respondents.

Table 5.9 Original and present main role of organisations

Type of service provided	Originally N	%	At present N	%
Umbrella organisation	19	9%	25	12%
Providing services	82	38%	88	41%
Providing self-help/mutual aid	29	13%	24	11%
Promoting community involvement	3	1%	3	1%
Providing information	14	6%	17	8%
Providing education or training	10	5%	10	5%
Promoting a cause	39	18%	30	14%
Promoting research	4	2%	2	1%
Cultural/hobby	8	4%	7	3%
Other	3	1%	3	1%
Professional organisation	7	·3%	7	3%

The two tables offer evidence that there has been an increase in provision of services across a majority of categories for all organisations. Decreases in the types of services offered as main roles of organisations have occurred only in two categories—providing self-help/mutual aid (13% to 11%) and promoting a cause (18% to 14%) (Table 5.9). However, there have been substantial increases in the provision of these services as subsidiary roles (35% to 45% in the case of providing self-help/mutual aid and 21% to 36% in the case of promoting a cause) (Table 5.10). Voluntary organisations are also more likely now to be providing education or training and promoting research as subsidiary roles than they were when they were originally set up (Table 5.11). Overall, the complexity and variety of services provided by organisations have increased considerably.

Table 5.10 Original and present subsidiary roles of organisations

Role of organisation	Originally		At present	
	N	%	N	%
Umbrella organisation	16	7%	24	11%
Providing services	50	23%	59	27%
Providing self-help/mutual aid	78	35%	97	45%
Promoting community involvement	55	25%	71	33%
Providing information	133	61%	139	64%
Providing education or training	102	46%	129	59%
Promoting a cause	64	21%	79	36%
Promoting research	75	34%	102	47%
Cultural/hobby	19	9%	25	12%
Other	0%	0%	1	0.5%
Professional organisation	0%	0%	0	0%

(note: respondents could provide more than one answer)

The growing complexity and broadening of service provision associated with the voluntary sector has taken place within a situation where the State (particularly in an Irish context) has increased statutory provision. The goal of community participation in the development of social services has had different degrees of impact in both voluntary and statutory agencies. The ethos and structures of many voluntary organisations has been changed by what Oliver (1996) has termed, in the context of the disability movement in the UK, a 'social movement'. At the heart of the transformation has been the rise in the number of organisations controlled and run by disabled people themselves. This social movement has proved effective in ensuring progress across a number of areas such as:

- specific legislation
- the creation of new organisations and institutions
- consciousness-raising and legislation
- internationalism
- human rights, civil rights and citizenship (Oliver, 1996: 43)

Although Oliver (1996: 43) acknowledges that these organisations have faced difficulties in terms of underfunding, lack of faith from policy-makers and professionals, opposition from traditional voluntary organisations and, finally, the presence of disabling environments in finding ways to communicate, meet and organise, their impact has been colossal in reshaping the organisational environments of the disability voluntary sector.

The influences identified by Oliver have been replicated across a wide variety of other areas, e.g. community development. This area has been described by Crickley and Devlin (1990: 53) in their overview of community work in the 1980s as a site for the solution of various social and economic issues, e.g. unemployment and the provision of care for those deinstitutionalised by health cuts. Voluntary organisations have readily embraced the concept of community involvement and adapted it to their own and their statutory funders' requirements.

Knight, in his comprehensive survey of the voluntary sector in the UK, has also found that 'social welfare' in its broadest sense was the most frequent activity of local voluntary groups. The social welfare function was followed by advice and information; education and training; recreation and campaigning. However despite the diverse nature of activities, Knight also found that 81% of local voluntary agencies were philanthropic, as opposed to 44% of those in poor areas (Knight, 1993: 86).

All the 16 organisations interviewed by UCC agreed that their range of services had expanded since their formation, reflecting the pattern of changes presented in Tables 5.9 and 5.10. A respondent from a housing advice agency observed that:

We had to develop and expand our services across different geographical areas because there was an obvious shortfall in other areas.

Another respondent, also active in the housing area in a shelter for homeless women, remarked that:

The demand for our services has increased considerably so we have been forced to upgrade our premises so the quality of the service can be improved. People who avail of our services expect a much more professional service. One of our new roles is to develop education services . . .

From comparing the results of Tables 5.11, it is evident that the isolationist nature of the activities of voluntary organisations has diminished considerably. A significant reason cited by respondents for their formation was the lack of any alternative organisation (statutory or voluntary) providing similar services. Nearly three-quarters of organisations (73%), when they were first formed, were in the business of providing services not provided by other voluntary organisations or by the State. This has dropped to 47% of organisations who are now providing services. This figure graphically reflects the dearth of statutory welfare in the early years of the State, or what has been described as the 'auxiliary role of the State' (Breen *et al.*, 1990: 41).

Voluntary organisations are significantly more likely to cite the inadequacy of the work undertaken by other voluntary organisations as a reason to justify their existence now, relative to reasons used to justify the original founding of the organisation. The survey found that 4% of organisations used this reason to justify their original foundation, in comparison to 9% of organisations who now use it to justify their present existence (Table 5.11). The overall increase in the awareness of other voluntary organisations involved in the same general activity illustrates, on one level, an increase in associational life, which has been identified by Landry and Mulgan (1995: 64) as a key feature of modernity (Landry and Mulgan, 1995: 64). On the other hand, competition between voluntary organisations for funding and public support has led to what Brenton (1985: 182) has described as the phenomenon of 'grantmanship', whereby organisations oriented their activities towards goals that they felt to be most financially rewarding. This may have the paradoxical result described by Rice (1992: 386–395) whereby 'agencies will seek to follow Government trends in order to secure finance and consequently the world of social welfare will become unitary and less varied'.

Table 5.11. Reasons why organisation was first formed and reasons for its existence in the present

	Originally		Present	
	N	%	N	%
The organisation was set up to meet a need which was not being met by any other organisation, either statutory or voluntary	160	73%	103	47%
Other voluntary organisations were carrying out similar work but not meeting need sufficiently	9	4%	20	9.1%
Statutory organisations were carrying out similar work but not meeting need sufficiently	2	0.9%	7	3.2%
Other voluntary organisations were already adequately meeting need and we aimed to supplement their work	1	0.5%	2	0.9%
Statutory organisations were already adequately meeting need and we aimed to supplement their work	0	0%	2	0.9%

(note: respondents could give more than one answer)

It is apparent from looking at the results of the UCC survey of voluntary organisations in Table 3 (Appendix 5) that the range of client groups has increased considerably since many organisations were founded. Each specific group of people was taken separately and the extent to which they are targeted by voluntary organisations in 1995 was tested against the extent to which they were targeted in 1975 (or year of formation, if later). None of the specific groups of people listed were targeted significantly more or less by organisations in 1995 than they were in 1975 (or year of formation). However, all the listed client groups in Table 5.13 had access to the services of an increased number of voluntary organisations. The greatest single increases were in the areas of children and women, but these increases just failed to be statistically significant. In 1975, or in subsequent year of formation, 17% of organisations were providing services to children. In 1995 this had increased to 24% of organisations. Other areas that had increased provision by voluntary organisations were services for women, for people with disabilities and for the unemployed. Under the category 'other', services provided by voluntary organisations included community development-type organisations (22 organisations supplied these services both in the year of formation and in 1995) and organisations to represent professional interest groups (7 organisations supplied these services in year formed and in 1995).

Ruddle and Donoghue, in their 1995 study of 250 voluntary organisations, found that the main client groups were elderly (45%), community in general (32%) and unemployed people (21%) (Ruddle and Donoghue, 1995: 27). The elderly also featured as a significant client group in the UCC research, for whom 18% of organisations provided services. A comparative study of voluntary organisations in 10 European countries (Ruddle and Donoghue provided the Irish component of the study) concluded that the Republic of Ireland had the most specialised organisations, while Bulgaria had the least. In four of the countries (Ireland, the Netherlands, Sweden and Great Britain) elderly people are the most common group (Gaskin and Smith, 1995: 75).

The identification of a broader set of needs and a wider target group corresponds with many of the organisational and development trends associated with voluntary organisations. Voluntary organisations have classically been described as providing many innovative actions, which are later taken on board by the State (Kramer, 1981). The broadening of interests reflects what many theorists call the emergence of new social movements. It also has major organisational implications for voluntary organisations in that funding and bureaucratic imperatives grow with organisational expansion.

Table 5.12 provides a summary of the main comments from respondents to an open question on the issues affecting changes in client groups. Of the small number of who responded (16% of the survey sample), the most common response was that the organisation had continued providing services for its original client group together with an expansion of services for other groups, and that the needs of both client groups had become increasingly complex (55%).

Table 5.12. Summary of comments regarding changes in the nature of client groups

Comment	N	%
Same target group but increased numbers	5	14%
Wider target group (i.e. same people plus different types of people)	12	33%
More complex needs/broader approach taken	8	22%
Wider target group plus more complex needs	20	55%
Change of emphasis	4	11%
Other	5	14%

Valid cases 36   Missing cases 187

The effect of the growing complexity of client group needs is also captured in Table 5.13, where respondents were asked to describe in their own terms the main changes that had affected their organisation since its formation. The largest changes experienced by most organisations can be broadly described in terms of organisational growth, combined with a larger number of diverse clients. The largest single response reflects increased confidence within the sector about organisations' abilities in meeting needs since their formation (19% of respondents believed that their organisation had increasing success in meeting its service provision aims). Negative changes since formation were captured by reference to a difficulty in recruiting volunteers (3% of respondents) and a shortage of funding (2%).

Table 5.13. Main changes experienced by organisations since formation

Changes	N	%
Growth – resources/staff/volunteers/number of clients	61	30%
Growth – broader target group/broader or increased services	14	7%
Dealing with more complex needs	5	2%
Change of emphasis of service provision	26	13%
Professionalisation of organisation	29	14%
Increasing success of organisation re aims/service provision	39	19%
Decreasing success re aims/service provision	4	2%
Decrease in interest in organisation/just a few volunteers doing all the work	7	3%
Other	18	9%
Decrease/shortage of funding	3	2%

Valid cases 206   Missing cases 17

Distinctive contribution of voluntary organisations

Discussion of the distinctive contribution of voluntary organisations is rarely focused by reference to relatively abstract values such as 'deepening civil society' or providing forums for the expression of what Giddens has called dialogic democracy. Giddens (1994: 17) argues that the democratic qualities of social movements and self-help groups come in large part from the fact that they can open up spaces for public dialogue in respect of the issues with which they are concerned. The results from the research provide evidence that a significant basis for the perceived success of an organisation's activity is provision of better social services. This result is derived from asking respondents to list the main success of their organisation at the moment. The answers are shown in Table 5.14, where over 30% of respondents cited increased service provision across a number of categories as being the main success of their organisation. Other successes cited included providing information (14%) and empowerment/mutual aid (11%).

109

Table 5.14. Main success identified by organisation

Main success at the moment	N	%
General service provision to children	4	2%
General service provision to young people	1	0.5%
General service provision to elderly	7	3%
General service provision to specific illness	8	4%
General service provision to specific need	9	4%
General service provision to physical disability	2	1%
General service provision to mental handicap/learning disability	7	3%
General service provision to homeless	6	3%
General service provision to geographical location	1	0.5%
General service provision to carers	1	0.5%
General service provision to women	1	0.5%
General service provision to others	16	8%
Lobbying	8	4%
Providing information	29	14%
Providing advice and support	17	8%
Training and education	17	8%
Community development/ integration...	8	3%
Empowerment/ self-help/mutual aid...	23	11%
Raising awareness re cause	24	11%
Research/funding research	1	0.5%
Other	15	7%
Developing/improving the organisation	8	4%

Valid cases 213   Missing cases 10

A highly distinctive contribution of voluntary organisations, identified in the research, refers to the level of contact with similar organisations in Northern Ireland. Nearly three-quarters of the respondents (74%) had some level of contact with organisations in N. Ireland (Table 5.15). In Table 5.16, the nature of the contact with organisations in Northern Ireland is presented, showing that 30% of respondents are organised on a 32-county basis. Other listed contacts include joint project work with clients, services or training (23%) and contacts based on affiliated organisational structures (38%). The extent of cross-border voluntary sector engagement demonstrates inherent capacities for an extension and a deepening of civil society independently of political structures.

Table 5.15. Contact of organisations with counterparts in N. Ireland

Contact	N	%
Yes	165	74%
No	58	26%

Valid cases 223

Table 5.16. Type of contact with organisations in N. Ireland

Type of contact	N	%
32-county organisation	48	29%
Joint projects/work re clients, services or training	37	22%
General contact with related/sister organisations	53	42%
Only contact is that organisation in ROI and sister organisation in NI are both members of international umbrella organisation	5	3%
Other	1	0.6%
Main objective of organisation is to work in N. Ireland or with N. Ireland groups	3	2%

Valid cases 163   Missing cases 60

Conclusion

This chapter has presented some conceptual discussion about the definition of voluntarism, the parameters of voluntary action, the institutions of the sector and distinctive contributions. There is evidence from the UCC survey of the general population that the volunteer section of the population has a stronger perception of the importance of community involvement and is less oriented towards possessive individualism. They also believe more strongly in a sense of shared values among the Irish population. Advocates of communitarianism and the strengthening of civil society believe that these value systems

111

underpin a vibrant voluntary sector.

The UCC survey of voluntary organisations and subsequent interviews also reveal that respondents believe that the voluntary sector embodies the spirit of civic participation. The majority of organisations surveyed were formed in the 1970s and had experienced considerable development in the provision of their own services. These developments reflect changing needs of clients as well as a tendency to provide services on the basis of social solidarity as opposed to beneficence.

Chapter 6: Voluntarism, Human Resources and Professionalisation

The role of the volunteer

President Mary Robinson, in her speech to Dáil Eireann of 9 July 1992, gave special attention to the role of the voluntary sector. After observing the vast range of activities undertaken by people through voluntary commitment, she went on to declare that:

> It is usual to lay these efforts at the door of pragmatic necessity; to say scarce resources makes them essential. I believe that this is an inadequate explanation. Having seen them, I am sure they are something much deeper and more constant in our identity. I see them as bringing together within a single vision of action both strong community values and distinctly Irish ones. (*Irish Times*, 10 July 1992)

The conception of voluntarism as a natural and intrinsic attribute, which develops from what Billis (1993: 159) has termed the 'personal world', where welfare is provided by relatives, neighbours and friends, to a more formal setting within a voluntary organisation is widely shared. The values attaching to voluntarism in Ireland have deep roots in pre-modern Ireland. Joyce and McCashin (1987) have written that the values attached to voluntary work have their basis in the traditional nature of social life in Ireland, particularly in the late nineteenth and early twentieth centuries. Rural social values were based on reciprocal social relationships and a strong community spirit. Joyce and McCashin (1987: 97) also highlight the impact of the lack of State social services as well as the role of the Catholic Church, which provided resources, both spiritual and material, that were vital to the development of the voluntary movement. Faughnan (1990: 26) points out that while religious organisations played a major role in the shaping of the voluntary sector, a tradition of self-help organisations also influenced the nature of the sector, in the particular the growth of Muintir na Tire in the 1930s. Voluntarism was given a major added boost by the emergence of the dairy co-op movement at the turn of the century and the growth of credit unions from the 1950s onwards (Faughnan, 1990: 26). From the 1960s onwards, emerging trends for the expression of voluntarism have been the community focus of non-Governmental intervention and the growth in self-help organisations.

Gaskin and Smith (1995), in their overview of the influences on the voluntary sector in the Republic of Ireland, also emphasise the strong Government commitment towards community care over the past three decades. Relative to other European countries, the Republic of Ireland was to the fore in its adoption of community care. This promotion of community care featured strongly in a number of reports, the most influential being the Report of the Care of the Aged in 1968, which led to a huge growth in voluntary Social Service Councils and Care of the Aged Committees around the country. Mr Erskine Childers, Minister of Health, in commenting on the establishment of the Cork Community Association Trust during this period, observed that:

> The establishment of social service councils working in close collaboration with the Churches and welcoming all volunteers and helpers in a country such as Ireland, where there is still a very marked collective conscience maintained by the influences of the Churches would perhaps stave off the deterioration of modern society so evident in the modern world. (CCDI Archives, Cork)

However, despite these developments and later pronouncements on the importance of voluntary activity in community care (e.g. *The Years Ahead – A Policy for the Elderly*; Department of Health, 1988), and the establishment of a number of funding mechanisms, concern has been expressed at the policy vacuum around voluntary work (Gaskin and Smith, 1995: 12). The most significant study of volunteering trends in Europe was the report entitled *A New Civic Europe: A Study of the Extent and Role of Volunteering* (Gaskin and Smith, 1995). This study examined the extent and role of volunteering in ten countries of Europe: Belgium, Bulgaria, Denmark, France, Germany, the Netherlands, the Republic of Ireland, Slovakia, Sweden and the United Kingdom. In their discussion of the concept and culture of volunteering, the authors of the report identify widespread general agreement on the basic concept of volunteering, which they describe as:

> activities or work done of a person's free will for the benefit of others (beyond the immediate family) for no payment other than in some cases a

small honorarium and/or expenses. (Gaskin and Smith, 1995: 7)

They also list some of the main factors that have influenced volunteering across Europe, including the following:

- *The Church*— As in Ireland, the origins of much of voluntary work lie in religion and this has affected both individual motivation and organisational development. In strongly Catholic countries the Church's role has been pronounced, particularly in Ireland where the principle of subsidiarity was promoted by the clergy as an alternative to State welfare, which was perceived as the thin edge of the socialist wedge (see Chapter 4).
- *Statutory volunteering*—Some countries have a tradition of involving people in an unpaid capacity in State-run and public organisations. In the United Kingdom an active minority of volunteers work directly for Government bodies, for example social services departments. A different type of statutory volunteering took place under communist regimes, where the State took over voluntary organisations and required citizens to participate in 'coerced' volunteering.
- *Organisational membership*—In Scandinavian countries the grounding of culture in popular mass movements has had a decisive influence on the voluntary sector. The best example of this is Sweden, where there has always been a strong membership of organisations committed to the interests of their membership as well as the common good.
- *Civic duty*—The concept of volunteering as a civic duty is exemplified to varying degrees throughout Europe. The best example is Germany where the concept of civic duty was enshrined in law early in the nineteenth century. 'Citizen obligation' has recently become criticised for its coercive flavour, and the term 'voluntary social citizen engagement', which allows for freedom of choice, is increasingly preferred. Civic duty also became a significant factor in the development of volunteering under communism where independent voluntary associations were abolished and 'voluntary' activities became obligations imposed by the State.
- *Social participation and status of women*—The role of women in volunteering, both past and present, is extremely important. The development of professional social work owed its origins in many European countries to the activities of middle-class women who saw volunteering as an expression of social status.

115

- *Relationship with Government* — A wide variety exists in Government's relationships with the voluntary sector across European countries. These range from close historical collaboration, as in Germany and Sweden, to the near stand-off in France and coercive relations under communism. Relationships have changed all over Europe with the recent shift in political perceptions of the role of voluntary work in the welfare system (Gaskin and Smith, 1995: 7-9).

The scale of voluntarism

According to Faughnan (1990: 22), the specific influences on the voluntary sector in Ireland reflect indigenous historical influences. Faughnan highlights the results of the Irish report on the European Values Systems Study undertaken in 1984, which showed that over half of the adults in the Republic of Ireland claimed membership of an organisation of some kind. This was high relative to the European average, but much of the higher membership was attributable to involvement in religious organisations. The Irish component of the European Values Systems Study also found that one in five in the Republic of Ireland claimed to be a voluntary worker. In comparison with the European average, activism in Ireland was high in charitable, religious and youth work fields, but low in relation to political parties and professional associations (Faughnan, 1990: 22).

The national opinion survey of the population carried out for the Social Studies Research Unit in UCC found that 32% of the national population had given services without pay to a voluntary organisation during some time in the past (Table 6.1).

Table 6.1. Percentage of population who had given services without pay to a voluntary organisation

	Services given without pay
yes	32%
no	68%

A breakdown of the volunteer population is provided in Table 1 (Appendix 6). The results of the research show that 48% of the population who had given services without pay to a voluntary organisation were men and 52% were women. Other interesting findings reflect the social class composition of volunteers. ABC1 classes (upper middle and lower middle classes) were more likely to have volunteered. 43% had given their services as volunteers, whereas only 25% of the skilled and unskilled working class (C2DE) had volunteered. Farmers featured midway between these two groups (34% had given their services without pay to a voluntary organisation).

The Leinster region (excluding Dublin) was the area where the population was most likely to volunteer (47% of the Leinster population as opposed to 24% in Munster and Connacht/Ulster. The level of volunteering in the Dublin region was 33%. Overall there was little difference between urban and rural areas as regards levels of volunteering. In rural areas, 33% of the population had offered their services without pay to a voluntary organisation, as compared to 34% in urban areas. Married people were more likely to volunteer than single people (36% of married people in comparison with 28% of single people). There was little difference between the volunteering levels of the population who have children and those who have no children. 30% of the population who have no children volunteered, as compared to 29% of the population with children aged under 5 years and 34% of the population with children aged between 6 and 14 years of age.

The age profile of the population who have volunteered reflects an over-representation of the 35–54 age group (42% of this age group have volunteered even though they constitute only 32% of the population). There are slight under-representations of the 15–34 age group (27% of this group have volunteered, even though they constitute 42% of the population). The participation rates of the 55+ age group are close to their representation levels in the population i.e. 26% and 28% (see Table 2, Appendix 6).

The results from the national opinion survey also show that 18% of the population are currently giving their services to a voluntary organisation (Table 6.2).

Table 6.2. Percentage of population currently giving their services without pay to a voluntary organisation

	% of general pop.
yes	18
no	82

In Table 3 (Appendix 6), this population of current volunteers is broken down. Whether an individual is currently giving their services to a voluntary organisation is highly significantly related to their age group and social class. The age group most likely to be volunteering is the 35–54 age group, of whom 25% are at present giving their services to a voluntary organisation. Only 14% and 15% of the other age groups were giving their services as volunteers. The Leinster region (excluding Dublin, which has the lowest at 13%) is the area with the highest levels of current involvement at 25%. Women were slightly more likely to be volunteering at present than men (19% as opposed to 17%). Middle class people were also more likely to be volunteering at present (24% for ABC1 groups as opposed to 14% for C2DE groups and 22% for farmers). There were also slightly higher rates of current participation in rural (22%) than in urban (20%) areas.

As part of the national opinion survey, respondents who were not giving their services to a voluntary organisation were asked whether they were willing to use their spare time for voluntary work. Overall, 65% of the population agreed with the proposal and 22% disagreed (Table 6.3).

Table 6.3. Percentage of population who are not currently giving their services to a voluntary organisation and willing to use their spare time for voluntary work

	% of general pop.
willing	65
don't know	13
unwilling	22

A breakdown of the population willing to use their spare time for voluntary work and who are not currently doing so is presented in Table 4 (Appendix 6). For those who are not presently doing voluntary work, their willingness to use their spare time for such work is highly significantly related to their age group. An individual's willingness is also related to the region in which they reside. Willingness is also related to gender and social class. There was equal support for the proposal from the 35-54 and the 55+ age groups (69%). Only 54% of the 15-34+ age group supported the proposal. The Leinster region was most in favour of the proposal, at 74%. The percentage of women not at present engaged in voluntary work and who supported the proposition exceeded the percentage of male non-volunteers (73% in contrast to 57%). ABC1 non-volunteer members of the population were the most supportive of the proposition (74% of the population in comparison with section C2DE of the population at 63% and farmers at 55%). The urban non-volunteer section of the population was most in favour (72%, rural non-volunteer section of the population 60%).

The UCC survey results are generally comparable to the results from the most recent national survey of volunteering in the Irish population: *Reaching Out: Charitable Giving and Volunteering in the Republic of Ireland*, the 1995 survey carried out by Helen Ruddle and Ray Mulvihill. Their survey of 1,000 respondents found that 35% had been involved in some kind of voluntary work (formal and informal) in the month prior to interview. 20% of respondents had carried out voluntary work through an organisation (formal volunteering) and 23% of respondents had carried out voluntary work on their own, not undertaken through any organisation (informal volunteering) (Ruddle and Mulvihill, 1995: 94). Ruddle and Mulvihill's figure of 20% for organised volunteering within the past month corresponds closely to the 18% response obtained by UCC for current levels of involvement.

The UCC research compares closely to some of the main findings by Mulvihill and Ruddle, such as:

- Women are more likely than men to be volunteers (39% of women had volunteered in comparison to 31% of men in Mulvihill and Ruddle's 1995 study).
- Those in the 34-55 age group were the most likely to volunteer. Ruddle and Mulvihill (1995) found that those in the age groups 51-60 and 41-50 were most likely to have given time to volunteering activity.

119

- Members of the ABC1 social classes were far more likely than the C2DE section of the population to have volunteered. Ruddle and Mulvihill (1995) used the reasonably equivalent variable of educational background to determine extent of volunteering based on class, and had similar findings to those of the UCC survey. They found that 70% of respondents with the primary certificate gave no time, compared with a half of those with third-level qualifications (Ruddle and Mulvihill, 1995: 60).

The propensity of the middle class and better educated sections of the population towards formal volunteering has also been captured in studies of voluntary affiliation in other countries. One such study of voluntary affiliation in six countries (USA, Canada, Britain, Germany, Italy and Mexico) found that volunteering was positively correlated with social class (Curtis, 1971: 872). In commenting on American research on the area, McPherson (1991) concludes that the class structure of America has an extremely important effect on the membership and involvement of various groups in the voluntary sector. McPherson (1991) proposes a model for interpreting this phenomenon based on the level of organisational affiliation related to status. In this model, high status people have more memberships of organisations than low status people. Low status people are more likely to drop out of organisations. It is likely, therefore, that high status individuals will experience a greater membership of different organisations during their lifetime. McPherson (1991) does not explain why this is the case, but it does reflect the general pattern whereby many voluntary organisations have relatively large numbers of middle class people (McPherson, 1991: 716).

The study of volunteering patterns undertaken in *A New Civic Europe: A Study of the Extent and Role of Volunteering*, published in 1995, also found a high degree of consistency in the demographic and socio-economic profile of volunteers across Europe. There was a marked tendency for volunteering to increase with social class, measured by level of education and type of occupation (Davis and Smith, 1995: 30–32). This study also found a high level of regular volunteering across the sample of eight countries. It found that two-thirds of people volunteer at least once a month, one-quarter less often, and one in ten said it varied or they didn't know. According to the findings of the study of volunteering in Europe, around one-quarter of Irish people had volunteered in the past year. Bulgaria, Germany and Slovakia had low rates of volunteering at

120

less than 25%, highest in the former East Germany and as low as 12% in the case of Slovakia. Belgium, Netherlands, Sweden and the UK had the highest levels of volunteering (Gaskin and Smith, 1995: 28).

Limits of voluntarism

Hedley and Smith (1992) have argued that voluntarism is facing a number of challenges due to changing social trends. These are:

- Demographic trends—the fall in the birth rate since the late 1960s means that there are fewer young people available to volunteer
- Economic trends—the entry of more women into the paid labour market means that fewer women are available to do voluntary work
- Social trends—the breakdown of traditional family structures. Married people are more likely to volunteer than single people. In the UK, single people made up only 10% of regular volunteers according to the 1981 volunteer survey. The breakdown of traditional 'close-knit' communities has also had an impact on volunteering. People are spending less time inside their neighbourhoods, both for work and for leisure (Hedley and Smith, 1992: 1–4).

Hedley and Smith (1992) also note the work of Stuart Hall in the UK, who has claimed that Governments are stealing the language of the voluntary movement—the language of self-help and consumer rights—in pursuit of their own philosophy of economic liberalism and of rolling back of the frontiers of the State. In a UK context, Government calls for an increase in voluntary activity have more to do with nineteenth-century views of philanthropy and charity than with the ideals and philosophy of the voluntary movement today (Hedley and Smith, 1992: 4).

In an Irish context, other trends, which are related to the concerns of the transition to a postmodernist society, have also become apparent. These include:

- the impact of the decline of traditional Catholic morality on charity
- increased scepticism towards public institutions such as the Dáil, politicians and the effectiveness of welfare services
- increased drive towards private satisfaction
- more popular social concerns such as the environmental movement and the self-help movement, which have affected the ability of older and more traditional service provision organisations (such as the meals-on-wheels organisations) to attract younger volunteers
- less adherence to traditional authoritarian structures

121

The broader challenges can also be identified within the difficulties faced by organisations in recruiting and retaining volunteers.

Table 6.4. Difficulty organisations had in obtaining services of volunteers

Degree of difficulty	N	% of organisations who responded
More difficult	72	39%
No change	86	47%
Easier	23	13%
Other	2	1%

Valid cases 183   Missing cases 40

Of the organisations that responded to the UCC survey, 39% had experienced difficulties in getting the services of volunteers (Table 6.4). This finding reflects the findings of Ruddle and Donoghue, who carried out a national study of 250 Irish voluntary organisations in the social welfare area as part of the Irish component of the study *A New Civic Europe: A Study of the Extent and Role of Volunteering*. Ruddle and Donoghue (1995) found that 42% of respondents had fewer volunteers than they required (Ruddle and Donoghue, 1995: vii).

Table 6.5 shows the issues identified by respondents to the UCC survey on the question of whether it is easier or more difficult to get access to the services of volunteers. The largest group of responses concerned a perception by 31% of organisations that it was hard to get interested people. It was also felt by 20% of respondents that it was difficult to get skilled people to become involved. The greatest concern in this regard was that volunteering was no longer very attractive or that people were reluctant to give their time. 11% of respondents felt that too many organisations were competing for volunteers.

Table 6.5. Comments of respondents about difficulty/ease of access to services of volunteers

Comment of respondents	N	% of valid cases
Too many organisations	10	11%
Cause not attractive	8	9%
Hard to get skilled people	18	20%
Difficult to get interested people	28	31%
Voluntary work is now considered too demanding	15	17%
Members are ill/old	6	7%
Cause more well-known	9	10%
Cause more attractive	2	2%
Organisation more known	11	12%
More people available	8	9%
Other	16	18%

(note: respondents gave more than one comment)

Nearly two-thirds of the respondents (62%) felt that the level of volunteering from the Irish population was adequate for their organisation's activities. 15% strongly agreed with this suggestion (see Table 6.6). This finding suggests that there may be a high degree of satisfaction within organisations with the level of recruitment. The consequence is likely to be a lower emphasis on recruiting additional volunteers.

A variety of opinions were elicited from respondents to the UCC postal survey regarding their perceptions of the key limitations of voluntarism. These limitations are shown in Table 6.7.

Table 6.6. Respondents who agreed/disagreed as to whether level of volunteering of Irish people was sufficient for organisation's activities

Respondents who agreed/disagreed	N	% of valid cases
Strongly agree	28	15%
Agree	88	47%
Disagree	66	35%
Strongly disagree	5	3%

Valid cases 187   Missing cases 36

Table 6.7. Main limitations of the use of volunteers identified by representatives of voluntary organisations

Issues identified by respondents on recruitment of volunteers	N
Recruitment of appropriate volunteers	4
Limited life of volunteers	3
Directing volunteers into appropriate activity	1
Training of volunteers	1

Typical of the views obtained from interviewed respondents, in interviews, were the following from a national youth organisation:

> *Youth work today is much more stressful, with increased levels of child abuse and youth suicide. It is harder to get committed people because of the difficulties youth workers face.*

The difficulty facing youth organisations in the recruiting and vetting of volunteers against a background of an increased awareness of the reality of child abuse was a particular issue identified by other organisations dealing with young people. But there were more general problems associated with the recruitment and retention of volunteers. The following responses are illustrative:

> *Volunteers usually last around 3 years in the organisation and work between one and a half and three and four hours weekly, depending on the branch. The expansion of our services will mean that we will have to rely less on volunteer input.* (respondent from organisation dealing with victims of crimes)

> *We have plenty of volunteers, however sometimes it is difficult to steer them into the boring activities such as doing the washing up in the café.* (respondent from

organisation dealing with youth homelessness)

> *We found that a lot of people were coming for the training course after being selected as volunteers and were then leaving as soon as it was finished. We decided to provide the course to all of the public, regardless of whether people wanted to become volunteers or not. Afterwards we asked the participants whether they wished to join the group as volunteers.* (respondent from organisation dealing with suffers from AIDS)

Issues raised by both the UCC survey of voluntary organisations and the intensive interviews identify some of the important variables on effective maximisation of volunteer effort within voluntary organisations. These variables overlap with some of the issues identified by Taylor (1996: 122) to maximise volunteer recruitment and retention. These are:

- selection/screening
- equal opportunities
- job descriptions/guidelines
- training and information
- regular support and supervision
- someone to talk about any problems or queries
- out-of-pocket expenses
- health and safety (including provision for safe transport)
- insurance cover

Level of professionalisation

The limits of voluntarism form part of what has been described by The National Institute for Social Work in the UK as 'philanthropic amateurism' (Leat, 1990: 236). This arises because voluntary agencies are poorly equipped to respond to the growth of professionalism. Not only do some voluntary agencies emphasise the use of volunteers, but insofar as they rely on contributions for their income they are in a poor position to attract professional staff.

Increasing professionalisation is an issue that goes to the heart of the voluntary sector. In effect it identifies an important divide in the voluntary sector between *voluntary agencies* and *volunteer organisations*. According to Billis (1993), who has suggested this distinction, large areas of voluntary activity fall between the personal, bureaucratic and association worlds. Ambiguity exists because some groups straddle the associational and bureaucratic worlds, referred to by Billis as 'ambiguous voluntary agencies', and some groups straddle the associational and personal worlds, referred to as unorganised groups. An association proper has therefore the attributes of legal identity and membership. According to Billis's framework, if the association employs staff only as a supporting role to the roles of the volunteers, e.g. secretarial staff or staff in the headquarters of a national organisation, it can be still be classified as an association. However, if the association employs paid staff to carry out its operational work, it has certainly ventured much more into bureaucratic territory and should be classified as an agency.

Billis points out that the move to bureaucratic forms means increased differentiation of roles and status, as categories such as 'member', 'committee member', 'volunteer', 'staff' and 'director' emerge. One of the results of these developments is the ambiguity of many of the degrees of status associated with these roles. This ambiguity is sharpened by the consequent tension between the formal characteristics of the bureaucratic world and the informal characteristics of the associational and personal worlds. The management of ambiguity in voluntary associations means that attention must be paid to the needs of bureaucracy, e.g. managerial authority and accountability, and to those of the association, such as informality and democracy (Billis, 1993: 160-164).

The clearest expression of this ambiguity is in the relationship between volunteers and professional staff. Kramer (1981: 206) has noted that it is 'widely believed there is an inherent conflict between professionalism and volunteerism'. Much of the literature on this aspect of voluntary sector employment focuses on the challenges involved in 'interweaving' the work of paid professionals and volunteers. Bulmer (1986: 214) has written that 'professional roles and the roles of informal care-givers are different, and there exist considerable problems in attempting to integrate the two'. There is evidence that different levels of status are accorded to professionals and volunteers, which curtail the level of collaboration between volunteers and staff. Difficulties in agreed work practices between volunteers and professional staff may also reveal themselves in allocation of roles. Darvil and Mundy (1984), drawing on studies of relationships between volunteers and social workers in Social Service Departments in Britain, found that volunteers work most with groups that social workers prefer to deal with least. Four reasons are offered for this reluctance on the part of social workers:

- there is an inadequate supply of volunteers
- there may be special problems in areas of high deprivation

- there may be a significant risk factor (e.g. working with children)
- direct contact with the client is better than organising volunteers or community resources (Darvil and Mundy, 1984: 6).

Despite increasing professionalisation of the voluntary sector however, certain characteristic features of voluntary sector employment result in its being sharply differentiated from comparable employment in both the private and State sectors. O'Donovan and Varley (1995), in their review of the literature, highlight four broad distinctive features of voluntary sector employment. These are:

1. the influence of organisational ideology on work relationships
2. the presence of volunteers who may work side by side with paid professional staff or serve on the governing bodies of voluntary agencies
3. the peculiarities of voluntary sector management practices
4. pressures exerted on voluntary agencies by heavier reliance on State funding (O'Donovan and Varley, 1995: 46).

In assessing the impact of these influences on the enormous diversity of voluntary sector employment, O'Donovan and Varley (1996: 46) have also suggested that there is a strong tendency for voluntary sector employees to find themselves trapped in a 'secondary labour market'. Primary labour markets are associated with high levels of pay, job security, good working conditions (resulting from strong unionisation) and the presence of an internal career structure. In contrast, in the secondary labour market, jobs are insecure and poorly paid, there is lack of organised unions and a failure to provide a career structure (O'Donovan and Varley, 1995: 46).

These 'secondary labour' characteristics of the voluntary sector in Ireland, already noted in chapter 3, have been magnified by the extensive use of Government employment schemes, particularly in their present form as Community Employment (CE) schemes. Under the CE programme:

> Public sector and voluntary organisations are grant-aided by FAS in respect of sponsoring a CE project and they in turn benefit in a secondary way by being able to carry out worthwhile work which they could not otherwise undertake. The programme is targeted primarily at the long term unemployed. Participants are generally engaged for a twelve month period for an average of 39 hours per fortnight.
>
> However some participants may be re-engaged for further periods with

the agreement of FAS where such participants are key participants and no other suitable eligible person is available or where the participant would benefit from additional training/development (Dept of Enterprise and Employment, 1997).

The impact of FAS/CE initiatives is considerable, given that 48,000 people are employed on the schemes and recruitment by voluntary organisations using the schemes has become very common. From the Government's point of view, the system has the advantages of reducing the unemployment figures and the provision of a training mechanism for the unemployed and a focus for community development in disadvantaged areas. For voluntary organisations, the schemes are useful because the organisation gets free staff for at least a year as well as funding for administrative costs. In reality, many organisations face the difficulties of ensuring that services provided under these schemes do not collapse when there is a mandatory turnover of staff.

O'Donovan and Varley's concept of the secondary labour market is even more pertinent when applied to CE workers within voluntary organisations. The use of CE workers has implications for the perpetuation of the low-wage economy within the voluntary sector. The working conditions of many CE workers may vary considerably because the bargaining position of these workers is far weaker than that of full-time workers, arising from the temporary nature of their employment, their lack of trade union membership and their expectation that full-time work may arise later. Finally, the effectiveness of CE schemes in providing full-time employment for participants remains open to question. An unpublished report for the National Economic and Social Forum in 1993 found that there were significant levels of unemployment among a sample of people six months after they finished a CE scheme (WRAC, 1993).

The evidence from the research undertaken by the UCC Social Studies Research Unit is, however, that a significant degree of professionalisation has taken place. This degree of professionalisation is reflected in the numbers of the population who state that they are employees of a voluntary organisation or who have taken part in Government-funded employment schemes.

In Table 5 (Appendix 6) there is clear evidence of the increasing organisational complexity associated with the voluntary sector. Organisations were asked to chart their progress in terms of whether the

128

numbers of staff (full-time and part-time), volunteers, members and clients/users of services had increased since their formation (from 1975 if organisation was formed before this date) as compared with 1995.

All voluntary organisations have experienced a very statistically significant rise in their numbers of all types of staff: clients; members, and volunteers. Nearly two-thirds (64%) of respondents had no full-time staff in 1975 or in the subsequent year of formation. This contrasts with 44% of respondents in 1995. Similar increases are evident in the use of part-time staff—84% of respondents said that in 1975 (or in the year of formation after this date) they had no part-time staff. This contrasts with 55% of respondents in 1995 saying they had no part -time staff. One of the biggest changes is in the area of the use of staff on employment schemes. One-third of organisations were using staff on Government-sponsored employment schemes in 1995. The increase in the use of these schemes corresponds closely with the beginning of their extensive development from the 1980s onwards. These changes also correlate closely with corresponding increases in the numbers of volunteers and clients. The results of the interviews indicate that some voluntary organisations see Community Employment Schemes as being essential to their ability to cope with increased demands (see Chapter 7).

The results of the national opinion poll also provide evidence of the increasing take-up of Government employment schemes by the labour force. As noted in Chapter 1, the results of the national opinion poll carried for UCC show that 2% of the adult population are employed by a voluntary organisation as part of a Government Employment Scheme. The survey also found that 2% of the adult population described themselves as employees of voluntary organisations[1] (Tables 6.8 and 6.9).

---

[1] The number of respondents detected in the survey is quite small (N = 51, employees of a voluntary organisation and N = 62 for employed by voluntary organisation on a Government employment scheme). Therefore the results must be interpreted cautiously.)

Table 6.8. Percentage of population who are currently employed by a voluntary organisation

	% of general pop.
yes	2
no	98

Table 6.9. Percentage of population who are currently employed by a voluntary organisation as part of a Government employment scheme

	% of general pop.
yes	2
no	98

Examples of the views obtained from the UCC survey, illustrative of the mindset that exists within the voluntary sector regarding roles and responsibilities, were as follows.

> *The volunteers perform invaluable roles such as dealing with telephone queries, fund-raising and some of the outreach work. However, all of the counselling work is done by professional staff.* (respondent from organisation dealing with rape victims)

> *With the use of CE schemes, we have been able to radically extend the range of services available. The schemes have enabled many volunteers to progress from volunteering, through CE schemes and on paid full-time positions in the organisation.* (respondent from organisation providing youth services)

> *Problems with the schemes include the difficulties caused when people leave the CE schemes. The schemes should be longer and there should be more consultation with FAS.* (respondent from housing advice organisation)

> *The people who miss out on CE schemes are those who need them the most. People with low levels of education and who have been unemployed for very long periods.* (respondent from community development organisation)

> *Staff are expected to do a lot more than staff doing similar roles in the Health Board. This is partly because the volume of work is so huge, and with so little*

resources and backup. (respondent from housing advice organisation)

Staff should never completely dominate an organisation. A strong voluntary board can act as a counter weight to interests of the staff. (respondent from housing advice organisation)

The evidence from the interviews suggests that overall there are very positive attitudes towards the implications of professionalisation for selected voluntary organisations. The evidence from the survey of organisations presents a general picture in which growth in the numbers of volunteers, members and clients corresponds closely with increased numbers of paid/professional staff.

Conclusion

Voluntarism has often been said to have a unique and distinctive place in Irish social life. This tradition has long roots in various Irish voluntary organisations, particularly those affiliated to the Church or based on community development principles. These factors affecting voluntarism in Ireland have common characteristics and are distinct from the wider European experience. Unlike other European countries, Ireland does not possess a history of statutory volunteering or the articulation of volunteering as a civic duty. In terms of the scale of volunteering, the research undertaken in this book supports earlier studies that approximately a third of the Irish population are active in some form of voluntary work. Earlier research confirms that the scale of voluntarism in Ireland lies within the middle range across a Europe-wide continuum. The research undertaken by the UCC Social Policy Unit confirms other international trends, which show a positive association between social class and volunteering. Other trends identified by the research reveal that the most likely group of volunteers are aged between 34 and 55 years.

Ireland faces limits on voluntarism based on changing social patterns such as changing demographic, economic and social trends. The UCC survey of organisations has found that 39% of a sample of 183 organisations had difficulties in recruiting volunteers. However, over half of the respondents felt that the level of volunteering within the Irish population was adequate for their organisation's activities. The effective maximisation of volunteer initiative raises a number of key organisational issues for voluntary organisations. Overcoming these difficulties reflects the degree to which a voluntary organisation has

131

associational or *agency* characteristics. The transition to an agency is clearly marked by the numbers of professional staff within an organisation.

The evidence from the survey of voluntary organisations is that professionalisation has made a big impact on the voluntary sector. Despite this trend, however, there is evidence that much of the employment within the voluntary sector is of a 'secondary labour market' or workfare nature—poor career structure, low pay, long hours and temporary employment. These features have become more pronounced with the extensive use of CE schemes by voluntary organisations.

Chapter 7: Role of Government and Statutory Funding of the Voluntary Sector

The relationship between the voluntary and the statutory sectors in Ireland has been a defining feature of Irish social policy for the past 20 years. A constant theme identified during this is the focus on the issues of fund-raising and participation in the decision-making processes that shape social policy. At one level the framework within which these issues are discussed has changed considerably, with the development of the 'partnership' approach towards the tackling of social problems. At another level, although the dependence of the voluntary sector on statutory funding has increased considerably, difficulties still persist in its adequacy and administration.

The publication in 1997 of the Green Paper by the Department of Social Welfare on the Community and Voluntary Sector and its Relationship with the State was the culmination of a process stretching over 16 years. Since 1981, organisations had been waiting for various Governments to publish a charter for the voluntary social services (Council for Social Welfare, 1991: 1). At a conference held in Galway in June 1990, entitled 'Partners in Progress, the role of the NGOs', the then Minister for Social Welfare committed himself to the preparation of a White Paper on the interaction between voluntary organisations and the State. According to Jaffro (1996: 11), the ostensible purpose of such a charter was to provide official recognition of the role of the voluntary sector in Irish social services. On the one hand the Government could expect, as a result of the proposed White Paper, more accountability and less duplication of services from the voluntary sector. At the same time voluntary organisations would expect to gain wider recognition by the Government and agreements with the State regarding core funding.

In 1996 it was announced by the then Minister for Social Welfare that in place of a White Paper, which would set out proposed legislation, a Green Paper would be published in 1997 which would open the door to discussions—to a forum where opinions can be expressed and recorded. The failure to produce a White Paper came as a major surprise to the many organisations that had either made submissions to the Dept of Social Welfare (the Department responsible for the drawing up of the Charter) or taken part in an advisory group that had drafted the major elements of the White Paper. Jaffro (1996: 11) has commented that the difficulties associated with the publication of the document reflect a lack of agreement between Government Departments on the definition of appropriate funding arrangements. Despite this lack of progress in policy, the diversity of funding mechanisms that have emerged in recent years reflects a transition from a model of voluntary/statutory relationships, based on *ad hoc* funding arrangements, to contractual or partnership-based approaches.

Official recognition of the potential of such approaches has been most recently addressed in the Green Paper (1997) from the Dept of Social Welfare. The objective, as noted above, of the Green Paper is to discuss a framework for the future development of the relationship between the State and the community and voluntary sector and to facilitate a debate on the issues relevant to that relationship. The Green Paper is the first systematic official overview of the issues facing the voluntary and community sector and the legal and political context within which it operates. It identifies the need to develop and support the sector at both local and national level. It also addresses the complex system of funding arrangements available to the voluntary sector from Government Departments and the EU. The Green Paper is also broadly in favour of developing mechanisms for gathering the views of voluntary organisations in the formation of policy. In the area of funding there is a clear recognition of the need for consistency in procedures for grant application.

Mulvihill (1993: 66–7) has characterised statutory–voluntary relationships as falling into four basic models, as follows.

- *Welfare pluralism* — associated with the administration of services by voluntary organisations where finance is provided by the State. The State and voluntary organisations in this model are expected to play different but interdependent roles in providing social services. Funding arrangements depend largely on commitments by the State to ensure widespread provision of social services.
- *New Right approach* — views the voluntary, commercial and informal sectors as substitutes for State provision and supports these sectors only as a means of realising the policy of 'rolling back the Welfare

State'. This approach is strongly associated with the development of 'contractual' relationships between voluntary organisations and the State.

- *Subsidiarity*—the principle that a larger unit assume functions only to the degree that the smaller units of which it is composed are less competent to do so. This approach is strongly associated with Catholic social policy and has recently been revived by the EU as a mechanism for achieving a balance between the centre and the periphery and for distributing public authority among different levels of Government.
- *Partnership*—this is the planned delivery of social services by the statutory and voluntary sectors, based on agreed co-ordination and participation in the decision-making process.

Elements of all these approaches are being debated in many other European countries. As Mulvihill (1993: 68) points out, the nature and extent of these approaches is shaped by particular historical, demographic and prevailing ideological currents–social democratic, conservative or liberal. Mulvihill argues that the model of the voluntary–statutory relationship that approximates most clearly to the provision of community-based services for the elderly in Ireland is welfare pluralism, combined with a strong element of subsidiarity. According to Mulvihill, this welfare pluralist approach is far from ideal with problems existing in relation to funding and participation in the decision-making process. As a response to these difficulties a more comprehensive partnership approach is favoured (Mulvihill, 1993: 68).

The difficulties faced by voluntary organisations relying mainly on funding from the health boards have been identified in an important contribution to the debate on the difficulties facing the voluntary sector, arising from study carried out by Faughnan and Kelleher of 42 voluntary organisations in the Dublin area and their relationships with the State. The study identified difficulties in three principal areas:

- funding relationships with the State
- ongoing contact with the State
- role of voluntary organisations in policy development (Faughnan and Kelleher, 1993: 17–21).

The principal difficulties in the area of funding were the lack of clarity as to the basis for grant allocation and the discretionary nature of the funding. Faughnan and Kelleher (1993: 19) write that:

Funding was frequently *ad hoc*, insecure, lacked a clear commitment by an appropriate State agency and failed to match the needs of the organisation. It was not so much the level or the amount of funding which caused most concern among voluntary organisations, but the framework within which it occurred.

The discretionary nature of the funding process is inbuilt into the principal mechanisms for the distribution of statutory funding to voluntary organisations in the social services, notably Section 65 of the Health Act 1953, which is one of the main funding mechanisms for many voluntary organisations. Under this Section 65, grants may only be paid by health boards in respect of 'services similar or ancillary to a service which the health board may provide' (taken from guidelines for grants to voluntary agencies under Section 65 of the Health Act, 1953). Faughnan and Kelleher (1993: 49), in commenting on these funding arrangements, write that:

> There appeared to be no pattern or coherence to the funding arrangements with the health boards. Historical precedent, access to key decision makers, political expedience and a measure of luck appeared to provide the basis on which the funding arrangements between individual organisations and the health boards were initially established and then consolidated.

Strategies proposed by the voluntary sector to respond to these difficulties can be generally considered to involve attempts to define clearly its role in relation to the voluntary sector. Despite the State's orientation towards funding voluntary organisations from the 1970s onwards under the rubric of community care, the failure to redress the inadequacies of the Section 65 legislation and the perceived deficits in policy participation proved crucial in preventing an equality of relationships as defined in an ideal welfare pluralist model. Sr Stanislaus Kennedy stated in her 1981 book *Who Should Care: The Development of Kilkenny Social Services 1963–1980* that by the early 1970s, the model proposed by the social service council movement had broken down. In this model, the services of statutory and voluntary organisations are co-ordinated by a local council made up of representatives of both sectors (Kennedy, 1981: 176).

136

The arguments in favour of joint consultation and planning and more formalised funding arrangements were actively promoted by a variety of writers from the voluntary sector. An example of this ongoing debate was the publication in 1982 by the National Services Board of a discussion document entitled *The Development of Voluntary Social Services in Ireland*. In the document, the NSSB argued for joint consultation and planning between statutory and voluntary bodies. Furthermore, it suggested that this joint consultation should take place at three levels:

- community or neighbourhood level
- community care area level
- health board level (Curry, 1982: 16).

Butler, writing in 1981, concludes that the failure to devolve power to the local level in Ireland has had deep-seated implications for the voluntary sector. Furthermore, the ability of local government to co-ordinate effectively with the voluntary sector was severely reduced by its loss of power. At the same time the co-ordinating mechanism for the voluntary sector—the National Social Service Council—was shunted into what Butler calls a 'limbo' because of ministerial inaction over its future (Butler, 1981: 16). In 1987, the NSSC was abolished and replaced by the National Social Services Board. The remit of this body was limited to the co-ordination of citizens' advice bureaux.

However in the area of community initiatives there has been a new commitment by the State which would seem to reflect a more localised partnership approach as compared to the more national visions of collaboration outlined by activists in the 1970s and 1980s, such as Kennedy (1981). Partnership is defined by the Irish Council for Social Housing as follows:

> [Partnership] therefore involves the formal introduction into the public administration system in Ireland of the role of properly constituted voluntary organisations operating effectively for community benefit and in the public interest, to bring the people and their communities or special interest groups, into the process of providing and managing their services for the common good. (Irish Council for Social Housing, 1991)

In relation to the social services, a partnership implies the creation of a 'third arm', which draws skills and resources from both the public and private sectors (Irish Council for Social Housing, 1991). In fact the novel aspects of the partnership approach towards community development in Ireland have been noted with considerable interest in an OECD

137

evaluation of the 38 Area Partnerships created by the Irish Government and the Structural Fund of the European Union, beginning in 1991. The OECD report describes the partnerships as follows:

> Legally the partnerships are independent corporations under Irish company law. Their boards bring together representatives of local community interests, including the unemployed, representatives of the national social partner organisations of labour and business, and local or regional representatives of the national social welfare, training or economic development administrations. They thus simultaneously pursue area-based economic development and the local integrated implementation of national programmes connected to it; and they do it in a way that blurs familiar distinctions between public and private, national and local, and representative and participative democracy. The preliminary results of this effort to foster development and welfare through new forms of public and private local co-ordination are quite promising, if still inconclusive. (OECD, 1996: 9)

The huge number of community initiatives (mainly stemming from financial support from the EU) which have received State funding has not prevented community activists and workers from recognising that significant problems exist in relation to the State's activities. These difficulties have been characterised by Lee (1990: 96), in her discussion of community links with the State in Ireland, as pertaining to:

- excessive centralisation and bureaucracy
- inefficiency and incompetence
- suspicion of its own constituent parts as well as of others
- vulnerable to direct action
- hi-jacking of community for its purposes
- politically and personally oppressive.

The new emerging complex interlinkages between the voluntary sector raise key questions about the role of the State. In particular, in light of the growing trend towards a partnership model and widespread acceptance that Ireland has a mixed economy of welfare, the clash between the reality of statutory/voluntary arrangements and their idealised workings within a welfare pluralist or partnership model becomes apparent.

The Green Paper (Department of Social Welfare, 1997: 48) recognises that practically all Government Departments provide funding to the sector: there is no overall Government policy on the role of the voluntary and community sector. Against this background, the Green Paper (Department of Social Welfare, 1997: 51) calls for the Government to recognise formally the voluntary and community sector and to outline a clear policy for its future role and development.

Funding and the State

Table 7.1 deals with changes in the approximate percentages of incomes derived from a variety of funding sources, both in the past and now. It is important to point out that the question in Table 7.1 deals only in percentages, as respondents were not required to provide detailed estimates of their funding. Also, some organisations may not have been aware that some of their statutory funding comes from National Lottery funds. A cautious interpretation of the mean figure is advised because of the high degree of standard deviation associated with the wide range of responses.

It is evident from the results in Table 7.1 that there have been overall increases in the contribution of European funding, statutory funding, direct receipt of National Lottery funds and charges for services to organisations' income sources. This is reflected in the greater absolute number of organisations obtaining funding from these sources as well as increases in their average mean percentage contribution to total income. The level of income from both European funding and the National Lottery remains very low, despite the increases. Decreases have taken place in the mean percentage contribution of membership fees and organised fund-raising, despite the increase in absolute terms of organisations using these income sources. The most significant increase in terms of magnitude relates to statutory funding. These results reflect the increasing reliance on the State for funding.

Table 7.1. Average percentage of income derived from the listed sources in 1975 (or the year the organisation was formed if after 1975) and 1995

Income source	Year	Mean	St dev	N
European funding	1975	1.26	8.1	168
	1995	3.57	10.03	182
Statutory funding	1975	16.99	31.38	167
	1995	23.34	31.24	181
Non-statutory funding	1975	8.97	23.91	165
	1995	8.92	20.48	181
National Lottery	1975	1.05	9.09	164
	1995	4.33	14.55	181
Membership fees	1975	22.25	36.38	163
	1995	17.02	30.45	180
Charges for services	1975	5.8	17.77	165
	1995	7.87	19.95	181
Organised fund-raising	1975	25.9	35.4	163
	1995	20.42	28.43	180
Personal donations	1975	12.15	24.38	163
	1995	12.13	23.68	180
Other	1975	2.52	12.66	164
	1995	2.33	11.34	180

Interviews with the 17 representatives of voluntary organisations have also shed light on a number of key concerns affecting reliance on statutory funding. These include some of the difficulties identified in a number of other studies, e.g. the previously referred-to research undertaken by Faughnan and Kelleher in 1993. These included the following.

Table 7.2. Issues raised by interviewees in relation to statutory funding

Number of interviewees	16
Terms of reference for receiving funding	4
Reliance on statutory funding conflicting with independence of organisation	2
Level of funding received	6

A respondent from a housing advice organisation cited the difficulties associated with balancing criticism of statutory sources and its possible effect on funding:

> *Question marks were placed over the core funding when criticism was voiced by the organisation over a particular Department's policy.*

Another respondent from a youth organisation believed that the State treated the funding requirements of the voluntary sector differently from those of the public sector:

> *The Dept of Finance would not index pay rates of staff in the organisation with those of the public sector, despite admitting that their particular role was indispensable.*

Organisations that were surveyed were asked to indicate how they would see the role of the State across a number of areas. In Table 7.4, respondents were asked to comment on whether or not the State should take a more direct role in providing the services of the organisation. 54% of respondents were in favour. Only 9% of respondents were against increased State involvement, and 37% were content with the present situation.

Table 7.3. Organisations' view of involvement of the State in providing their activities

Preference for involvement of State	N	%
More	91	54%
Less	16	9%
Same	63	37%
Valid cases 170	Missing cases 53	

141

The results in Table 7.4 indicate that the vast majority (88%) of organisations are seeking increased State funding for their activities. Table 7.5 shows the views of respondents towards the role of the State in monitoring the performance of organisations. 53% of respondents were content with the present level of monitoring, with 40% of respondents in favour of an increased regulatory function for the State.

Table 7.4. Attitude of organisations towards State funding of their activities

Preference for State funding	N	%
More funding	175	88%
Less	4	2%
Same	21	10%

Valid cases 200   Missing cases 23

Table 7.5. Organisations' perception of the role of State in monitoring performance.

Preference for State role	N	%
More	67	40%
Less	12	7%
Same	89	53%

Valid cases 168   Missing cases 55

Table 7.6. Organisations' perception of role of State in training staff/volunteers

Preference for State role	N	%
More	76	47%
Less	11	7%
Same	73	46%

Valid cases 160   Missing cases 63

In Table 7.6 it is shown that there was a generally positive reaction towards the benefits of statutory involvement in meeting the training needs of the voluntary sector. 47% of respondents were in favour of an increased State commitment in this area.

A large percentage of respondents (56%) were opposed to increased co-ordination/communication with statutory agencies. However, 45% of respondents were in favour of increased co-ordination with statutory agencies (Table 7.7).

Table 7.7. Organisations' preference for increased co-ordination/communication with statutory agencies

Prefer increased co-ordination	N	%
Strongly agree	13	7%
Agree	74	38%
Disagree	85	43%
Strongly disagree	25	13%

Valid cases 197   Missing cases 26

Table 7.8. Organisations' perception of their ability to impact on decisions of State

Level of power	N	%
A lot	16	8%
Some	66	31%
A little	69	33%
None	60	28%

Valid cases 211   Missing cases 12

The results from Table 7.8 show that 61% the organisations felt that they had little or no power in relation to the decision-making policies of relevant statutory organisations. This result is surprising given the promotion of 'partnership'. In effect, the welfare pluralist model is still prevalent where there still exists a strict demarcation between funding of an organisation (welfare pluralist model) and contribution to the decision-making process (partnership model).

The evidence from the 16 interviews also indicates a complex set of attitudes towards the role of the State. All the organisations interviewed were of the opinion that considerable expansion of the statutory services

143

was required to cope with social problems. None of the organisations were of the opinion that this expansion would obviate the need for their continued existence. A general response from four interviewees was that partnership, in the form of closer co-operation and co-ordination with the State, was good, but needed to be treated with caution so as to protect the independence of the voluntary sector. The opinion of a representative of a community development organisation is typical:

> Partnership can be a dubious concept if it means that voluntary organisations lose their ability to fight for the people they are supposed to represent.

Five of the respondents were very positive towards the possible introduction of contracts as mechanisms to stabilise statutory funding arrangements as well as ensuring greater monitoring by funders. One respondent, representing a federation of mental handicap organisations, explicitly welcomed the introduction of contractual arrangements:

> The use of contracts could be good for the voluntary sector. It would ensure far greater accountability and improve standards for the users of services.

In terms of specifying roles of the voluntary sector and the State in terms of their meaning for citizenship, one respondent representing a federation of organisations providing disability services argued that:

> Social rights are best ensured by the activities of the State. Civic duty is much more bound up with the activities of the voluntary sector.

The results of the research provide evidence that increased reliance on EU and Government for funds is a reality for much of the voluntary sector. The Green Paper (Department of Social Welfare, 1997: 47) provides an extensive breakdown on the substantial amount of funding—approximately £487 million annually—which it receives from the State and EU sources. This increased financial reliance is just one part of a broader picture, in which the welfare pluralist approach is being reshaped by the influence of partnership and contractual relationships. The policy of contracting out services is intimately associated with the privatisation of welfare, which is part of the retrenchment of the Welfare State. Privatisation, according to Johnson (1987: 17), means at its most basic a reduction in the role of the State and the transfer of some of its functions to private institutions (Johnson, 1987: 17). The private institutions may be commercial organisations, voluntary organisations or the informal sector. Johnson identifies three broad areas of State

144

intervention which, if they are reduced, constitute privatisation. These areas are:

- provision
- subsidy
- regulation.

Culpitt (1992: 97) writes that policy initiatives such as the contracting or privatisation of social services are attempts to redraft both the structure and the vision of welfare society. They are not just technical managerial issues and cannot be seen simply as procedures for the efficient delivery of services. Its adherents believe that the 'private' sector is the answer to the deficiencies caused when Governments supply social services. The successful application of social service contracting requires the specification of contracts and support for competition in service provision. The underlying logic of these policies draws heavily on the philosophies of the market place, the argument being that even a regulated private sector is more efficient than the public sector (Culpitt, 1992: 98).

In contrast, opponents of social service contracting have argued that the concern with efficiency has had serious effects for the provision of welfare. Culpitt (1992: 101) has written that:

> There are broader concerns of the social market that the pursuit of profit does not enhance. The pursuit of profit, for example engenders little compassion for the economic circumstances of others and hardly cultivates the individual sacrifice for the common good. Stringent concerns for economic efficiency give short shrift to interests in the adequacy of social provisions. Thus welfare for profit poses a delicate issue for the mixed economy of welfare. The delivery of social services may to some extent benefit from the inclusion of profit oriented activity. But if such activity is not embraced selectively and with great discretion, it may undermine the values and distort the communal value of the social market.

The fear that the pursuit of profit might encourage values inimical to the values of altruism and service to others reflects a long-standing tradition that universal statutory provision is morally superior to reliance on commercial provision (Mishra, 1981: 15). It has also been argued that the evidence does not support the view that a considerable increase in contracting out could result in more cost-effective measures (Webb and Wistow, 1986: 88). Other difficulties arise in establishing and managing systems of accountability and formulating and providing coherent social policy, because privately contracted welfare services are either fragmented and inadequate or wastefully competitive. The difficulties associated with taking on contracts can be seen, however, as going to the core of the welfare pluralist debate. They touch fundamentally on whether or not the advantages of voluntary sector provision can be transferred into a situation where it assumes a primary responsibility for social services. Three different kinds of disadvantage have been identified by a number of writers (for example see Brenton, 1985 and Kramer, 1991). The primary disadvantage is the excessive bureaucratisation created in trying to meet Government monitoring standards.

Considerable organisational efforts are needed to ensure that contractual guidelines are adhered to and that public funds are accounted for. This can lead to a huge increase in formalisation and bureaucratisation within the organisation. This results in an imitation of the formalistic attributes ascribed to State agencies, thereby negating the special advantages associated with voluntary organisations (e.g. flexibility).

A second disadvantage is that the reliance of voluntary organisations on public funding places them in a vulnerable position in an era of Government cutbacks. Brenton (1985: 182), writing about the British voluntary sector, has identified the phenomenon of 'grantmanship'. Organisations orient their activities towards the contracts they feel are most rewarding rather than allowing their own interests to be the determinant of their activities. The funding of voluntary organisations, whether by grants or payment for contract service, is still the expenditure of public funds and is therefore subject to the same criteria as are used to assess all Government expenditure.

The third principal problem is the possible loss of autonomy of voluntary organisations once contracts are entered into with Government. Kramer has pointed out that this advocacy function is one of the important functions of voluntary organisations. He goes on to say that 'the distinctive advocacy functions can be restricted to the advocacy of self-interests through continuous lobbying for higher rates and fewer regulations' (Kramer, 1991). Fear of losing contracts may result in a fear of explicitly attacking Government policy .

For voluntary organisations, the option of service contracting offers immediate advantages because they are sure of financial support from Government. It removes the extreme vulnerability faced by organisations seeking private funding. The advantages of a specific contract may allow them to concentrate their services on a particular clientele. They also have the possibility of generating their own funding and thereby improving their services. The public image generated by obtaining a contract can help in getting private funding and the involvement of volunteers. The involvement of volunteers may also increase the options for innovative styles of work. Close working relationships between the State and the voluntary organisation may provide opportunities for a greater impact on Government decision-making.

Discussion of these issues is an important reminder that moving the basis of statutory funding of voluntary organisations away from a relatively simple welfare pluralist model to one based more on the principles of partnership and contracts has implications for the very definition of voluntary activity. The issue of developing formalised funding arrangements is central to the Green Paper (Department of Social Welfare, 1997) on the voluntary and community sector. The further development of the partnership approach is also implicitly addressed in the report *Better Local Government – A Programme for Change* (Department of the Environment, 1996), where there is further discussion of the possibility of the integration of local Government and local development systems (including voluntary organisations).

Against this background, the reliance of voluntary organisations on statutory funding will become subject to increasing scrutiny, whether through involvement with EU funding, the development of a partnership approach or the approximation to a contract culture in an Irish context. The Green Paper (Department of Social Welfare, 1997: 53) has also called for policy implementation across funding agencies with regard to financial accountability procedures. At the same time the reliance on private fund-raising still remains an important feature of the debate over the funding of voluntary organisations.

Dependence on private fund-raising

Private fund-raising independent of statutory sources is a vital necessity for most voluntary organisations. On one level, private fund-raising is clearly a response to the inadequacies of statutory assistance for voluntary organisations. On the other hand, for neo-conservatives, private fund-raising represents, like active citizenship, a non-statutory financial alternative to meeting welfare needs. Leat (1995: 158) has written about the UK experience, where successive Conservative administrations have encouraged the voluntary sector to stand on its own feet, attempted to wean voluntary organisations off dependence on statutory grant aid and encouraged funding from other sources. Wilson (quoted in Leat, 1995: 159) has written that:

> Such a philosophy assumes that support of the voluntary sector is seen as very much a concern of the community at large rather than a primary concern of Government via the traditional grant-making process. Responsibility for voluntary sector support is laid firmly at the door of both commercial organisations and individual private givers.

This idea that other sources of funding will take up the slack created by Government withdrawal is misplaced. Rochester (1995: 28) argues that there appears to be little scope for increases in the contributions to be expected from charitable trusts and foundations, corporate donors and the traditional methods of raising donations from individuals.

A general response to the difficulties in securing funding from these sources has been the trend among many organisations to hire professional fund-raisers, with its implications for smaller organisations and those representing less popular causes. The role of professional fund-raisers and their remuneration has also attracted public concern. The Costello Report (1990: 111), which investigated fund-raising activities for charitable purposes, states that there 'exists a certain degree of resistance in acknowledging the employment of professional fund-raisers'.

In the most recent analysis of the role played by the National Lottery, carried out by Harvey in 1995, it was stated that as a result of its success in generating sales of almost £300 million a year, the National Lottery had been criticised for the size of its prize fund and for undermining the fund-raising efforts of existing charities. Harvey also refers to complaints that poor people disproportionately play the lottery; that it operates without sufficient public control; and that there are no criteria or procedures for its allocation. Finally, Harvey refers to the criticism that the Lottery has become in effect a political fund, allocated according to the preferences of Government ministers (Harvey, 1995: 7).

The results of the survey of organisations on their perceptions of the difficulties in obtaining donations from the general public are shown in Tables 7.9 and 7.10. In Table 7.9 it is shown that 54% of the organisations that responded were of the opinion that it was increasingly difficult to obtain voluntary donations from the general public. The most common complaint cited by organisations in Table 7.10 was the intense competition faced in the fund-raising market, leading to donor fatigue (42%). The pressures created by other professional fund-raisers were cited by 11% of respondents, and 23% of respondents cited the effect of the National Lottery. On the other hand, 43% of respondents noted positive changes in their fund-raising experiences; 12% believed that the increased professionalisation of their fund-raising strategies was a positive development, and 9% of respondents believed that their aims and objectives were now better known.

Table 7.9. Perception of organisations on whether it is more or less difficult to obtain donations from the public

Level of difficulty?	N	%
More difficult	83	54%
No change	55	36%
Easier	17	11%

Valid cases 155   Missing cases 68

Table 7.10. Comments on voluntary donations

Selected comments of respondents	N	%
Too many other charities competing, causing donor fatigue	42	42%
Too many other charities using professional fund-raisers	10	10%
People prefer to buy National Lottery tickets	23	23%
Cause not popular/well known	11	11%
Change in people's attitudes	4	4%
Change in people's ability to give money/time	13	13%
Number of members decreasing	1	1%
Tapped same sources too often	6	6%
Growth in work–more need to fund-raise and less time to do it	6	6%
Cause is more well known	9	9%
Organisation is more professional/well known/ experienced	12	12%
More potential sources	2	2%
Other	14	14%
People believe their donations are wasted on administration	6	6%

Valid cases 100   Missing cases 123

In Table 7.11, the organisations surveyed were asked to comment on whether or not they believed the level of donations they received from the public was adequate. Of those who responded, 40% felt that the level of donations was not adequate and 60% disagreed with this proposition.

Table 7.11. Number of organisations that felt that donations of Irish people were not adequate

Level of donations is not adequate?	N	%
Strongly agree	23	12%
Agree	52	28%
Disagree	80	43%
Strongly disagree	30	17%

Valid cases 185   Missing cases 38

From the results in Table 7.12, the majority of organisations surveyed (64%) believed that the National Lottery had no impact on the financial position of their organisation. Respondents who believed that the National Lottery had an effect were split equally (18% each) between those who considered it had negative and positive consequences. Attitudes towards the effect of the National Lottery are considered more fully in Table 1 (Appendix 7) in which respondents explored further their attitudes towards the effects of the National Lottery. 20% of respondents cited the positive effects of the Lottery, because it provided a new source of funding which in some cases is easier to access than other sources. 20% of respondents cited negative effects of the Lottery, mainly due to its impact on their fund-raising attempts from the public. 4% of respondents were of the opinion that overall the Lottery had little effect because it simply substituted for statutory funding.

Table 7.12. Effect of National Lottery on overall financial position of the organisation

Any effect?	N	%
Yes, positive	37	18%
Yes, negative	37	18%
No effect	132	64%

Valid cases 206   Missing cases 17

A number of the interviewees raised concerns about both the difficulties attached to private fund-raising and dependence on the Lottery. One respondent from a housing advice organisation observed that:

> It is increasingly difficult to get public donations because of the tremendous competition between organisations. Especially so because of the number of professional fund-raisers employed. It is also difficult because people are asked to fund things like schools and hospitals which were previously funded by the State.

Another respondent from a Travelling organisation dealt with the issue that certain causes are not popular with the general public:

> For an organisation like us which represents Travellers, it is virtually impossible to obtain funding from the public in the form of collections or sponsorship from the business sector.

For one representative of an organisation in the disability sector, Lottery funding had changed the way the public felt about donations:

> The National Lottery has changed the way the public feel about donating. Firstly there is less money to donate because of the expenditure on tickets, and secondly there is a feeling that there is a lot more money available to the voluntary sector which in reality is not the case.

A representative of an organisation in the youth sector referred to what she considered to be the erosion of secure funding by dependence on Lottery funds:

> Funding for the Youth Affairs Section is coming primarily from the Lottery. This has eroded State funding and made future reliance on the statutory funding more insecure for voluntary organisations.

Donations provide one of the most obvious expressions of support for the voluntary sector. The willingness to donate draws on universally held definitions of virtuous behaviour, which Martin (1994) describes as 'morally desirable ways of relating to people, practices and communities'. According to Martin (1994: 5), 'the virtues centre on caring for others as well as for oneself'. Economic theories of giving have also been advanced, such as the contribution of charity to an increase in public well-being or utility—one person's utility is said to increase when another person becomes better cared for in some way.

Evidence of a decline in the willingness of the public to donate is viewed with concern by both charities and advocates of civil society, if it signifies a lack of public concern for the welfare of individuals or the wider community in general. Such a concern is expressed in the most recent report of the UK Charities Aid Foundation, which publishes an annual league table of the voluntary sector's fund-raisers. The report found that people are giving less to charity. The trend away from giving is most marked among young people. The authors calculated that in 1974, 34% of households gave every fortnight, in contrast with 29% of households in 1997 (*The Guardian*, 30 June 1997).

The most extensive national research to date carried out on the factors affecting donations in Ireland is the 1993 study undertaken by Ruddle and O'Connor, *Reaching Out: Charitable Giving and Volunteering in the Republic of Ireland*. The research found that 89% of respondents had given at least once to charity in the month prior to interview. The research also found significant correlations between amounts donated and respondents' occupations and levels of disposable income. Respondents gave to charity for a number of reasons, the most outstanding being how deserving was the cause and whether it was local (Ruddle and O'Connor, 1993: 100).

In Table 7.13, figures from the UCC commissioned national opinion survey demonstrate that almost equal proportions of the population feel morally obliged to donate money to voluntary organisations (47%) and feel no such obligation (46%). However, a significantly higher sense of moral obligation is associated with the volunteer population (57%) than with the non-volunteer population (40%). Whether an individual feels morally obliged to donate money to voluntary organisations is highly related to whether or not they have had involvement with voluntary organisations.

Table 7.13. Percentage of population who feel morally obliged to donate money to voluntary organisations

	% of general pop.	% of pop. who have had involvement with voluntary organisations	% of pop. who have had no involvement with voluntary organisations
agree	47	57	40
disagree	46	39	50

In Table 7.14, just over a third of the population (37%) express the opinion that they are fed up with voluntary organisations always asking them for donations. The volunteer section of the population is slightly less inclined to express such an opinion (33% of volunteers vs. 40% of the non-volunteer population). Whether individuals feel fed up with voluntary organisations always asking them for donations is highly related to whether they have had involvement with voluntary organisations.

Table 7.14. Percentage of population who are fed up with voluntary organisations always asking them for donations

	% of general pop.	% of pop. who have had involvement with voluntary organisations	% of pop. who have had no involvement with voluntary organisations
agree	37	33	40
disagree	55	61	52

Conclusion

Resourcing of the voluntary sector is an indicator of emerging models of statutory intervention in civil society (transition from simple welfare pluralism to the partnership model). Despite the changes in the way the State is working with the voluntary sector (in the form of EU-funded regional partnerships) and the diversity of funding available from statutory sources, traditional barriers are still firmly in place in many areas, as evidenced by the results of the UCC research. The survey of voluntary organisations showed that there were strong preferences for increased State funding and an increased statutory monitoring role. However, difficulties still exist in relation to influencing statutory policy. The Green Paper on the voluntary sector also raises the possibility of formalising funding arrangements on the basis of an approximation of the contract system, as used in the UK. The introduction of this approach raises a complex set of questions relating to the introduction of commercial values into social services.

Dependence on private fund-raising has always had considerable appeal to neo-conservatives as part of their vision of a diminished Welfare State. The UCC survey of organisations identifies difficulties faced by organisations in attracting donations. At the same time there would appear to be an acceptance that the demands of the public are already stretched by numerous appeals for donations. The majority of organisations estimated that the National Lottery had no effect on their fund raising activities, although their detailed responses suggested a more complex view.

Nearly half of the population felt a moral obligation to donate money to voluntary organisations. This sense of obligation was positively associated with volunteering. Experience of volunteering was negatively associated with criticism of voluntary organisations for their constant search for donations. These findings would seem to indicate that a civic activity in one area (volunteering) supports and confirms a civic activity in another (donating).

Chapter 8: Effectiveness, Accountability and Governance of the Voluntary Sector

Efficiency within the voluntary sector

Voluntary organisations are sometimes criticised for being inefficient because they lack the drive to control costs in the manner of profit-oriented organisations. However as Knapp (1996: 167) argues, to discuss the concept of efficiency properly it is helpful to use the mixed economy of care framework to introduce issues concerning effectiveness. In an Irish context, Faughnan (1990: 3) has pointed out that as they operate in the social services field in Ireland, voluntary organisations resist concise classification, and that they comprise:

> self-help groups, organisations which provide material services, those offering information, advice and counselling as well as those engaged in advocacy and in development work. There are voluntary organisations which address the needs of the elderly, the poor, the disabled, the homeless, the unemployed, travellers, single parents, emigrants, those with addiction problems, children and youth.

A diversity of organisational forms predominates, as noted in Chapter 1. Against the reality of the diverse nature of the voluntary sector, discussion of effectiveness assumes comparative advantages of cost-effectiveness, choice, flexibility, innovation, participation by users and other citizens, campaigning and advocacy (Knapp, 1996: 172). The possibilities for the realisation of these advantages depend mainly on the perspective adopted by different stakeholders—the public sector, the voluntary sector itself and volunteers.

The debate over the relative advantages of the voluntary sector goes to the heart of the welfare pluralist/mixed economy of welfare approach to social services. Much of the available evidence, however, would indicate that the potential effectiveness of the voluntary sector may not be as self-evident as previously thought (see e.g. Kramer, 1981). The divergence between rhetoric and reality can be seen across three areas: choice, flexibility and innovation and cost-effectiveness.

Choice—Within the rhetoric of welfare pluralism, a clear role is seen for the voluntary sector in offering distinctive services and choice. However, as many critics have pointed out, the potential dangers associated with statutory funding arrangements include a narrowing of choice within the voluntary sector. This difficulty is particularly associated with the onset of a contract culture as implemented in the UK and Australia—regulation can force organisations to be more like each other rather than providing a choice. In an Irish context, arguments in favour of the choice-providing role of the voluntary sector are firmly established in many official discourses (see e.g. *The Years Ahead*, Department of Social Welfare, 1988). However discussion of the relationship between choice and the voluntary sector in Ireland must also reflect the reality that difficulties exist in public access to many professional social services in general (whether provided by the statutory or the voluntary sector). For example, as O'Mahony pointed out in her seminal 1981 study of the voluntary sector in Co. Mayo, services for the elderly provided by voluntary organisations are concentrated in an urban environment and elderly residents in rural areas are severely disadvantaged in access to both voluntary and statutory services (O'Mahony, 1981: 171). The discussion of choice in a situation where users are left largely to their own devices is meaningless.

Flexibility and innovation—The assumptions of voluntary sector flexibility and innovation are also central to the discourse of welfare pluralism. The validity of these assumptions has been challenged on the basis of international research (Brenton, 1985; Kramer, 1981; O'Donovan and Varley, 1995). Kramer has argued strongly that innovation in social service provision is as strongly correlated with public service agencies as with voluntary organisations. The implications of the 1996 OECD report on the Area Partnerships in Ireland would suggest that the collaboration between voluntary and statutory sectors can evolve to new forms of innovative structures, with possibilities for enhanced participation by the community. The survival of these innovations within the ADM structures will also depend on Government perception of the risks associated with innovation.

Cost-effectiveness—The argument that voluntary organisations have lower costs than their statutory equivalents features strongly in the lexicon of welfare pluralism (see Hatch, 1980; Gladstone, 1979). The evidence for this must however be tempered by the fact that, as shown

157

by this research, many voluntary organisations are increasingly looking to the State as their primary source of funding (see Chapter 7). This means in effect that voluntary organisations are another conduit for the expenditure of public funds. Lower costs in the voluntary sector have also been maintained by the reliance on what were identified in previous Chapters as 'secondary labour markets' (lower salaries and more insecure working conditions for staff) and 'workfare' (use of CE schemes).

Awareness of these variables, which determine efficiency, has been discussed in previous chapters dealing with the values of the voluntary sector (see Chapter 5). From the interviews, it is apparent that there is strong support for the argument that the voluntary sector can operate in a highly innovative fashion. A representative of a childcare organisation observed that:

> Statutory agencies are restricted by laws and the general requirements of bureaucracy. We can operate with far more flexibility and immediacy.

A representative from a youth organisation observed that:

> In general, I think we make far more efficient use of our money in contrast to the health boards. Our costs are kept to a minimum and every penny is accounted for.

A housing advice organisation respondent commented that:

> The voluntary sector represents choice. People have a choice on how they want to spend their money through donations and secondly the voluntary sector represents choice in social services.

Another important dimension of the debate about the effectiveness of the voluntary sector is its degree of internal co-ordination. This dimension is also an important feature of the welfare pluralist debate (e.g. the Wolfenden Committee Report (1978) in the UK, which advocated strong intermediary structures for the co-ordination of the voluntary sector). Faughnan, in her 1990 overview of the voluntary sector in Ireland, presented representative and co-ordinating organisations as comprising a distinct category of voluntary activity (Faughnan, 1990: 11). Faughnan describes a variety of umbrella organisations existing in a number of social service sectors (at both national and regional level) and offering a variety of functions such as co-ordinating and lobbying functions. The nature of the relationship between member bodies and umbrella organisations formed part of Faughnan and Kelleher's 1993 study of voluntary organisations in Dublin. This concluded that the relationship between member bodies and umbrella organisations was not without problems:

> It could be difficult to get individuals with a strong impact and profile within their own organisations to work together effectively. (Faughnan and Kelleher, 1993: 92)

The prospects for an umbrella organisation for the voluntary sector in Ireland have most recently been considered by Harvey in a report published in 1993. The research in the report tested the level and nature of support for a national umbrella body for the voluntary sector in Ireland on the basis of interviews with national voluntary organisations and a survey of fifty community organisations in Co. Galway. Harvey found that:

- two-thirds of national bodies, organisations and experts expressed support for a national umbrella body
- in the smaller community organisations support was much higher, at 85% (Harvey, 1993: 1).

Arguments in favour of a national umbrella body are that it would: (1) formalise links with Government and achieve cohesion in the voluntary sector; (2) expand the resources going into the voluntary sector; (3) enable strategic planning to take place; and (4) provide services not now available. Arguments against the relationship are that a national body would be 'captured' by Government and become an instrument for public policy (Harvey, 1993: 1). Harvey also points out that useful lessons may be learned from similar experiments in national umbrella bodies for the voluntary sector in Scotland and Denmark. The results of the UCC research in Table 8.1 show that the majority of respondents (56%) believed that the present levels of co-ordination/communication among voluntary organisations could be improved.

The concern with present levels of co-ordination is apparent despite the large number of organisations represented in the survey (see Chapter 5) that have affiliated branches.

159

Table 8.1. Organisations that agree/disagree that co-ordination/communication with voluntary organisations working in the same field is inadequate

	N	%
Strongly agree	19	9%
Agree	97	47%
Disagree	79	39%
Strongly disagree	9	4%

Valid cases 204   Missing cases 19

All the respondents either were affiliated to co-ordinating organisations or were co-ordinating organisations themselves (three of the respondents had co-ordinating roles for other organisations). The value of affiliation to an intermediary organisation was strongly advocated by those respondents that were themselves constituted on the basis that they would represent member organisations. These organisations saw themselves as providing support in the form of staff training, carrying out research and lobbying Government. The value of membership of intermediary bodies for the other organisations was also strongly advocated by all the other respondents.

Public perception of standards within the voluntary sector and the implications of accountability

The issue of standards, as the Report of the Commission on the Future of the Voluntary Sector (1996) (UK) points out, is important for voluntary organisations of all sizes. The report argues that concerns about reliability, availability and consistency can be important for volunteers and users alike (Report of the Commission on the Future of the Voluntary Sector, 1996: 104). The issue of standards may mean different things for different stakeholders. Describing the UK experience, the Report emphasises the lack of a national regulator of standards, performance or effectiveness that applies to all voluntary bodies. This is despite the extensive use of contracts as mechanisms of funding between voluntary bodies and statutory agencies. The issue of standards is also bound up with the expectation that users and professional staff will be involved in their development.

In the Irish context, many voluntary organisations have responded to the emerging concept of performance measurement. This is particularly the case with larger organisations where more systematic patterns can be developed, e.g. in assessing performance in terms of *outputs* and *impact*— thus reflecting the growing influence of a managerialist ethos in the voluntary sector. The effect of such measurements can be more patchy in a smaller organisation, where standards may not be formalised. The influence of statutory agencies on the formalisation of standards within the voluntary sector has varied considerably.

As discussed in Chapter 7, the funding relationship between the health boards and voluntary organisations, based on the Section 65 legislation of the Health Act, 1953, has no national criteria for expected standards or performance from voluntary organisations. On the other hand, the influence of EU evaluative mechanisms on funding arrangements for agencies such as Combat Poverty, the Department of Social Welfare and local partnerships makes meeting standards (e.g. user involvement) a key determinant of a project's success.

Tables 8.2 and 8.3 provide evidence that there is strong positive perception of the effectiveness of the voluntary sector in Ireland and its adherence to high standards of service. In Table 8.2, just over three-quarters of the population (76%) agree that voluntary organisations usually deal with people who use their services in a fair, open and honest way. Volunteers are more strongly in favour of the proposition than non-volunteers (80% vs. 73%). However, support for the effectiveness of voluntary organisations among the population is not significantly related to whether or not they have had involvement with voluntary organisations.

Table 8.2. Percentage of population who believe that voluntary organisations usually deal with people who use their services in a fair and honest way

	% of general pop.	% of pop. who have had involvement with voluntary organisations	% of pop. who have had no involvement with voluntary organisations
agree	76	80	73
don't know	13	7	17
disagree	11	13	10

In Table 8.3, based on the UCC national opinion survey, one-fifth of the total population agree that voluntary organisations have a poor record in solving the problems of the people they try to help. 61% of the population as a whole disagree with this proposition. Disagreement with this negative perception of the voluntary sector is expressed by 56% of the non-volunteer section of the population, in contrast with 71% of the volunteer section of the population.

Table 8.3. Percentage of population who agree/disagree that voluntary organisations have a poor record in solving the problems of the people they try to help.

	% of general pop.	% of pop. who have had involvement with voluntary organisations	% of pop. who have had no involvement with voluntary organisations
agree	20	20	21
don't know	19	9	23
disagree	61	71	56

The principal source of concern in the public perception of voluntary organisations relates to perceived inadequacies of the existing statutory controls over fund-raising activities for and by charitable and other organisations. This was evident from the research reported by Ruddle and Mulvihill in 1995. In this study—which was a follow-on from the 1990 report, *Reaching Out: Charitable Giving and Volunteering in the Republic of Ireland* (Ruddle and O'Connor, 1993)—it was found that 42% of the respondents felt that charities are not sufficiently accountable to the public for how the money given to them is spent (Ruddle and Mulvihill, 1995: 98). The most recent expression of Governmental concern was the setting up of an Advisory Group on Charities/Fund-raising Legislation, which submitted its report in 1996. The aim of the report was to examine the recommendations of the Costello Report of 1989. The Advisory Group Report agreed with the principle of registration of charities and that fund-raising by non-registered organisations should be prohibited. Other recommendations included calls for mandatory publication of reports and accounts by registered organisations. It also recommended that all accounts and contracts entered into should be open to public inspection, and a system of registration with the Charity Commissioners of professional fund-raisers (Advisory Group on Charities/Fund-raising Legislation, 1996: Appendix III). Legislation is currently being prepared to deal with the implementation of these regulations.

The concern with the financial probity of the voluntary sector reflects ongoing difficulties in the definition and meaning of the concept of accountability. Rochester (1995) has written that demands for accountability pose more difficult and complex issues and problems for voluntary agencies than for their counterparts in the private and statutory sectors. Private or profit-making organisations can be characterised as being accountable to their owners—the shareholders— and regulated by the market. Statutory agencies operate within clear and explicit terms of reference, which are defined in law. They are also organised hierachially both internally and in relation to one another. By contrast, voluntary agencies are held to be accountable for their activities in a number of different ways by a variety of constituents or stakeholders—members, beneficiaries, paid and unpaid staff, donors, Government and other funding bodies, the 'community' and the taxpayer (Rochester, 1995: 191). Leat (1995), who pioneered the concept of multiple accountability within the voluntary sector, has provided three basic distinctions:

Types of accountability—this involves (a) *full accountability* which is the right to demand an account and impose penalties if the account or the actions reported in it are deemed unsatisfactory, (b) *explanatory accountability* is a weaker form which confers the right to require an account, but not to impose sanctions and (c) *responsive accountability* where those seeking accountability do not have any clear rights and are dependent on the willingness of those responsible to take their views into account.

The right to acquire accountability—this involves (a) *structural accountability* which is derived from social or organisational structures— parents and children; managers and workers (b) *delegate accountability* is created by specific acts of accountability where somebody acts on behalf of somebody else and is accountable to this person for their actions and (c) *communal accountability* ,which is derived from a feeling on the part of those who are accountable that they owe accountability to some 'community' of

163

others with whom they identify.

Different areas over which accountability is exercised—this involves (a) for the proper use of money, *fiscal accountability*, (b) for following proper procedures, *process accountability*, (c) for the quality of work, *programme accountability*, (d) for the relevance and appropriateness of the work, *accountability for priorities*. (Leat, 1995: 193).

In an effort to assess the awareness of accountability, respondents to the UCC survey of organisations were asked to assess the adequacy of the voluntary sector's accountability to funders and clients/users. In Table 8.4, over half of the respondents (52%) strongly disagree that there is enough accountability to funders. Only 7% agree with the proposition. On the other hand, 95% of respondents agree that their organisation has adequate accountability to clients/users (Table 8.5).

The concerns expressed by voluntary organisations over the degree of accountability to funders partly reflects the failure, as already stated, to regularise the criteria for receipt of statutory funding by voluntary organisations. This concern over the proper use of money (fiscal accountability, to use Leat's phrase) has featured as a significant sub-text in the negotiations between the voluntary sector and the State. The other elements in Leat's dissection of accountability, have been less explicitly addressed by many voluntary organisations (notable exceptions are organisations in the disability and community sectors). This is partly a result of the complexity of internal organisational structures, affecting Leat's definition of accountability.

Table 8.4. Organisations that agree that there is adequate accountability to funders

	N	%
Strongly agree	6	3%
Agree	8	4%
Disagree	76	41%
Strongly disagree	96	52%

Valid cases 186   Missing cases 37

Tables 8.4 and 8.5 show that there is a highly significant difference between the extent to which voluntary organisations feel that there is

164

adequate accountability to clients and to funders. 95% of respondents agree that accountability to clients is adequate, whereas only 7% feel that the accountability to funders is adequate.

Table 8.5. Organisations that agree/disagree that there is adequate accountability to clients ·

	N	%
Strongly agree	90	44%
Agree	107	51%
Disagree	9	4%
Strongly disagree	3	1%

Valid cases 209   Missing cases 14

Governance, management and democratisation within the voluntary sector

In the Toquevillian tradition, the link between voluntary associations and the inculcation of democratic ideals in society is particularly strong. This position has been reaffirmed in much of mainstream sociology, where associations have been seen as social integrating forces: as intermediary bodies between individuals which counteract the processes of fragmentation and individualisation in modern society. In political science, voluntary associations have been seen as political integrating forces: as intermediary organisations between the individual/groups of individuals and the State. They help the processes of articulation and aggregation of interests in society (Dahl, 1971; Fukuyuma, 1995). One of the most undisputed theses in the study of political culture, therefore, is the relationship between political culture and democracy. Putnam, who has written extensively on the subject, has distinguished between the external and the internal democratic effects of democratisation. The external effects are related to the role of association in the processes of articulation and aggregation of interests. The internal effects are related to the effects on members of associations. These effects can be attached on the one hand to *mobilisation* (development of collective resources and political participation) and on the other to *democratic socialisation* (voluntary associations create habits of co-operation among their members, a sense of concern for public affairs and a sense of mutual

165

respect and acceptance) (Putnam, 1993: 89–90). The possibilities for voluntary associations to act as carriers of these democratic values become problematic if they function more as professional enterprises than as membership-based organisations.

This question brings to mind Croft and Beresford's (1986: 5) assertion that participation is an issue which tends to be long on rhetoric and short on information. However, the democratic associational model of voluntary organisations assumes that members should be not only expected, but actively encouraged, to participate in the running of the organisation (Lansley, 1996: 76). The quest for participation has become a feature of both statutory and voluntary agencies. The implications of participation raise a host of issues relating to the definition of user involvement (Taylor, 1996: 57). The use of the term 'user' has been modified by many organisations—both statutory and voluntary—to reflect the influence of the 'customer/consumer relationship'. The concept of customer may not always provide the best basis for users/members to have a direct say in the running of the organisation. The application of democracy across a variety of differentiated organisational types (e.g. the basic distinction between organisations run By Us For Us and organisations run By Them For Us) must also require an elastic definition of what is meant by user control of an organisation.

In Table 8.6, two-thirds of respondents believed that there had been no change in the level of democratic participation within their organisations. 32% of respondents believed that their organisation was more democratic in 1995 than in 1975.

Table 8.6. *Organisations that felt they worked in a more/less democratic way in 1975 (or the year founded, if after 1975) compared to 1995*

More/less democratic?	N	%
More democratic in 1995	58	32%
Less democratic in 1995	4	2%
About the same	121	66%

Valid cases 183   Missing cases 40

The mechanisms identified by respondents by which their organisations had become democratic were as follows.
- 18 organisations referred to the holding of meetings/elections to

committees.

- 12 organisations referred to the participation of clients/members in running services and contributing to the administration of the organisation.
- 8 organisations said the rights of users were taken into account and they were consulted.
- 4 organisations referred to the participation of workers and volunteers in the running of the services of the organisation.
- 1 organisation stated that there had been a move from the founders' sense of ownership to a more democratic approach within the organisation.

In Table 8.7, 41% of respondents believed that their clients/users/members had a lot of influence within their organisation, and 38% that they had some influence. The remaining 21% of respondents admitted that their clients/users/members had little or no influence.

Table 8.7. Organisations' perception of the level of influence of clients/users/members on decision-making within organisation

Influence of clients/users/members?	N	%
A lot	80	41%
Some	73	38%
A little	23	12%
None	18	9%

Valid cases 194   Missing cases 29

Table 8.8. Organisations' perception of the influence of volunteers on decision-making within the organisation

Degree of influence?	N	% of valid cases
A lot	120	64%
Some	28	14%
A little	21	11%
None	20	11%

Valid cases 189   Missing cases 34

In Table 8.8, nearly two-thirds of the respondents (64%) believed that their volunteers had a lot of influence on decision-making within the organisation. 15% said their volunteers had some influence, 11% a little influence and 11% no influence.

Many voluntary organisations are working with two models for the control and management of such organisations. The first of these is a managerialist professional model. Here the concerns are with securing the agency's mission in the most efficient manner, with consideration of consumer demand interpreted by those running the organisation. In this model the place of members and volunteers is determined by the contribution they can make to the effective running of the organisation. Members mainly contribute to the organisation by their fees and the legitimacy they add. Members may join executive committees. However these posts are often as likely to be filled from the outside, through direct recruitment of people with specialised skills (e.g. financial). On the other hand, many voluntary organisations are working within a democratic associational model where, as previously stated, members/users are not only expected but actively encouraged to participate in the running of the organisation.

Davis Smith (1996: 187) has suggested that the time is ripe to take stock and review developments over the past decade, asking the question whether management cultures imported from the paid workplace are appropriate for voluntary agencies. The key question here, as Lansley (1996) points out, is that the move to managerialism appears to allow little room for a philosophy that is centrally concerned with democratic involvement. He comments:

> Managerialist voluntary organisations will by all means listen to the members if what they have to say helps the agency to improve the product, count their numbers if that increases legitimacy, or use them as volunteers, but the members have no clear place within the organisation. (Lansley, 1996: 79)

The democratic associational model is, however, evident in the voluntary sector. It is sometimes referred to as the New Social Movements. These include such broad movements as feminism, anti-racism, peace and anti-nuclear campaigning and environmentalism. Lansley (1996: 79) describes social movements as rejecting economic values and hierarchical structures, and a common theme in many of these movements is personal experience of alienation from mainstream economic and social structures. The reality of the voluntary sector is a lot more complex than a simple bi-polar model of member involvement. The involvement of members in an organisation depends greatly on a range of factors, such as size, complexity, centralisation, ideological commitment and constitutional factors. However, as Lansley (1996: 79) also points out, these are dynamic as well as structural issues. The issue of membership involvement often becomes most apparent when there are value gaps between managers and members. It is also important to emphasise the role that ideology can play as a determinant of member participation—organisations seeking to promote new social values such as environmentalism are more likely to create strong pressure for user involvement than organisations that promote existing social values.

Faughnan and Kelleher's 1993 study of voluntary organisations in the Dublin area included an analysis of the forms of participation present at an operational level. It found that in more than three-quarters of the relevant organisations at least some formal mechanisms designed to promote participation by consumers were in place. In almost a quarter of the organisations no such mechanisms were indicated by respondents (Faughnan and Kelleher, 1993: 107). The evidence from the UCC survey of voluntary organisations also highlights the commitment of the majority of voluntary organisations to improving the involvement of volunteers in the running of the organisation. On the other hand, there was a much weaker sense that overall democratisation had improved greatly within the organisation.

All but one of the organisations had some form of representative structures, which were indirectly or directly accountable to the membership. The exception was a Church-based organisation, which operated through parish structures and whose director was responsible to the archbishop. The types of structures advanced by representatives of organisations as evidence of member involvement included the following from a representative of a housing advice organisation:

> An annual general meeting is held where everybody who has had involvement with the organisation comes together. The purpose of the meeting is a general discussion of the issues, e.g. direction etc. However before the meeting the committee itself holds a meeting where all the real decisions are made. The committee is not elected as such but consists of individuals who have a strong interest in the organisation's work.

Organisations that had a federated structure had a much clearer governance structure. A representative of a youth organisation described its national committee in the following terms:

> The national committee is made up of delegates from each of the regional branches, as well as other individuals co-opted on to the board.

The issue of users being represented on the board was quite clear to one interviewee:

> The board is dominated by parents of deaf people. There is only minimal representation from the deaf people who use the services. This has affected the priority given to the needs of older deaf people.

Empowerment, community development and equal opportunities

Parallel to the growing use of the language of user involvement and partnership, there has been an emphasis on the empowering role of voluntary organisations. Taylor (1996: 56) has provided a useful three-fold definition of the empowering role of voluntary organisations:

- user empowerment within the sector
- empowering users in the wider service arena
- empowering citizens.

The concept of empowerment incorporates a diverse range of approaches. In a study carried out in the UK in 1995, voluntary organisations came up with the following approaches when asked how they empowered users (Taylor, 1996):

- caring: alleviating suffering, freeing people from anxiety
- consumerism: mechanisms to keep users informed, seek user views and give them access to redress
- development: building users' capacity as individuals to control their own lives
- mutuality: gaining confidence through shared common experience
- solidarity: demanding a greater say as citizens and seeking to change power relationships in society.

The emergence of user empowerment poses a direct challenge to more traditional service provider organisations. A possible response to the demand for user empowerment is 'consumerist', which may be more common than 'democratic' approaches, which involve users in governance. A genuine user voice in services will require more than satisfaction surveys and an individual complaints system. The legitimacy of governance is often at the very heart of demands for empowerment. This has implications for both governing bodies and professional staff, for whom change can be a difficult process.

Traditional service provider organisations are themselves responding to the challenges posed by user-led organisations, which are sometimes represented as inspiring a 'silent revolution' in response to the traditional approaches of statutory and voluntary agencies. (Parker and Froland, 1983). The constraints faced by user-led organisations are in many respects similar to those faced by all smaller voluntary organisations. These include the dangers of formalisation attached to the use of contracts etc.

In Table 8.9, just over half of the respondents felt that their organisation had empowered clients/users/members to a greater degree than in 1975 or subsequent year of foundation.

Table 8.9. Organisations that empower clients/users/members less or more in 1995 compared to 1975 (or the year founded if after 1975)

More/Less empowerment?	N	%
More in 1995	86	51%
About the same	83	49%

Valid cases 169   Missing cases 54

The evidence from the survey of organisations is that a significant minority of respondents (44%) believed that there was a greater promotion of self-help/mutual aid within their organisations than in the past, while 54% of respondents believed that there had been no change within their organisation (see Table 8.10). Similar strong orientations are evident in the findings from the survey of organisations dealing with questions of working with community groups and promotion of equal opportunity policies. The results from Table 8.11 show that 43% of organisations have adopted policies which encouraged particular groups to use their services. Similarly 53% of organisations are working more closely with community organisations now than in the past (Table 8.12).

Table 8.10. Organisations that promote the ethos of self-help/mutual aid more/less among clients/users/members in 1975 (or the year it was founded if after 1975) compared to 1995.

More/Less promotion of the ethos?	N	%
More in 1995	78	44%
Less in 1995	3	2%
About the same	98	54%

Valid cases 179   Missing cases 44

Table 8.11. Organisations that use equal opportunity policies to encourage particular groups to use their services more in 1995 compared to 1975 (or the year founded if after 1975)

More/Less encouragement?	N	%
More in 1995	57	43%
About the same	75	57%

Valid cases 132 Missing cases 91

Table 8.12. Organisations that promote working with local community groups more in 1975 (or the year founded if after 1975) compared to 1995

More/Less promotion?	N	%
More in 1995	78	53%
Less in 1995	9	6%
About the same	61	41%

Valid cases 148   Missing cases 75

Conclusion

Discussion of effectiveness in the voluntary sector often assumes comparative advantages of cost-effectiveness, choice, flexibility, innovation and participation by users and other citizens. On the other hand, the possibilities for organisational and service provision innovation are largely determined by external factors such as the availability of public financing as well the nature of the service provided. The evidence from the UCC research is that these perceived advantages are closely linked to how many organisations see themselves, and that a very strong positive perception of the voluntary sector is held by the general public. The UCC research found that voluntary organisations also recognised that there were problems in relation to the existence of adequate accountability to funders (both public and private).

The association between the voluntary sector and democratisation and civic participation is also quite pronounced in the literature. The UCC research found that although the concept of democratisation was important to organisations, two-thirds of respondent organisations said that they had not changed significantly over a twenty year period (or since they were founded) in relation to this variable. At the same time, the majority of organisations believed that clients and volunteers had considerable influence on the organisation. There was also evidence of a strong orientation in many organisations towards using the concept of 'community' and the targeting of specific groups as a strategy for the planning of new services.

The focus on participation and user involvement is a vital contributory factor to what has been termed the 'associational revolution'. This will pose one of the biggest challenges to the voluntary sector as we enter the twenty-first century.

Conclusion

A central argument of this book is that modern society is increasingly characterised by detraditionalisation and individualisation. However, postmodern society, despite its tendencies towards fragmentation and polarisation, is also seen as the precursor to an invigorated civil society. The exponents of civil society view reciprocal responsibility and mutualism as the basis of civic virtue. A reinvigorated civil society is presented as an appropriate response to contemporary social problems. At the core of a revitalised civil society are intermediate institutions such as family networks, interest groups and voluntary organisations.

A central objective of this book has been to locate discussion about voluntarism, the parameters of voluntary action, the institutions of the sector and distinctive contributions firmly in the context of an evolving civil society in Ireland. Traditional conceptions of civil society are changing in response to a voluntary sector that in many respects is redefining itself. The UCC research has provided evidence that many voluntary organisations are increasingly adopting the philosophies of community development and empowerment and mutating into democratically based bottom-up communitarian organisations, and that attitudes supportive of civil society are widely held among the Irish population, particularly among those who have had involvement with voluntary organisations.

There is evidence from the UCC survey of the general population that the volunteer section of the population has a stronger perception of the importance of community involvement and is less oriented towards possessive individualism. Volunteers also believe more strongly in a sense of shared values among the Irish population. Advocates of communitarianism and the strengthening of civil society believe that these value systems underpin a vibrant voluntary sector. In terms of the scale of volunteering, the research undertaken in this book supports the finding of earlier studies that approximately a third of the Irish population are active in some form of voluntary work. The research undertaken by the UCC Social Studies Unit also supports international

studies that show a positive association b
volunteering. Other trends identified by the rese
likely group of volunteers are aged between 34 anc

The evidence from the survey of voluntary
professionalisation has made a big impact on the
Despite this trend, however, there is also evidence
employment within the voluntary sector is of a 'se
market' or workfare nature—poor career structure, low p   rs
and temporary employment. The growing confusion betwe   orkfare
(under the guise of CE schemes) and voluntarism threatens to violate the
basic ethic on which the latter rests.

Increased resourcing of the voluntary sector is an indicator of
emerging models of statutory intervention in civil society (transition
from simple welfare pluralism to the partnership model). Despite the
changes in the way the State is working with the voluntary sector (in the
form of EU-funded regional partnerships) and the diversity of funding
available from statutory sources, traditional barriers are still firmly in
place in many areas, as evidenced by the results of the UCC research.
The survey of voluntary organisations showed that there were strong
preferences for increased State funding and an increased statutory
monitoring role. However difficulties still exist in relation to influencing
statutory policy. The Green Paper on the Voluntary Sector also raises the
possibility of formalising funding arrangements on the basis of an
approximation of the contract system, as used in the UK. The
introduction of this approach raises a complex set of questions relating to
the introduction of commercial values into social services. The UCC
survey of organisations identifies difficulties faced by organisations in
attracting donations. At the same time there would appear to be an
acceptance that the demands of the public are already stretched by
numerous appeals for donations. The majority of organisations estimated
that the National Lottery had no effect on their fund-raising activities,
although their detailed responses suggested a more ambivalent view.

The evidence from the UCC research would also indicate that a very
strong positive perception of the voluntary sector is held by the general
public. The research found that voluntary organisations recognised that
there were problems in relation to the existence of adequate
accountability to funders (both public and private). The association
between the voluntary sector and democratisation and civic participation

pronounced in the literature. The majority of organisations …eved that clients and volunteers had considerable influence on their policy-making.

The voluntary sector is at a crossroads in terms of its role and direction. The Green Paper outlines a strategy for the voluntary sector where its relationships with its statutory counterpart are based on the emerging principle of 'social dialogue'. This presupposes the development of an enabling State which is engaged in dialogue and partnership and which allows bottom-up responses to emerge from voluntary organisations and community groups. This ideal form of a responsive and enabling State envisages a realistic transition in the relationship from 'separate dependency' to 'integrated dependency'. The implication of such a relationship is that it represents an incorporation of the voluntary sector by the State, with the attendant dangers of formalisation, based on the necessity of consensus politics.

The future contribution of the voluntary sector to an enhanced civil society in Ireland will depend greatly on the ability of the voluntary sector to respond imaginatively to the challenges posed by both closer co-operation and dependence on the State and the encroachment of for-profit principles derived from the influence of the commercial sector. The relevance of many voluntary organisations in contemporary Irish society will also be tested by their ability to adjust to a postmodern society, where the requirements of reflexive modernisation are increasingly felt in demands for accountability and user lead initiatives from within organisations.

In the transition to a postmodern society, the challenge of social policy is to respond reflexively to changing needs and demands. The challenge to universalist welfare is based on the particularism associated with identity politics and social movements—including neoconservative elements stressing the primacy of the market, the communitarian aspects of social obligation and the alleged inefficiencies of direct State intervention. The dilemma facing a disparate voluntary sector is how to reconcile its existence with the demands of common citizenship, previously associated with universalist welfare measures.

What will be the role for voluntary organisations in building a civil society inclusive of the less well off? This is the great social, political and intellectual challenge of postmodernity. The challenge of deepening civil society requires a discourse that is capable of dealing with the realities of the changes in social, personal and economic relationships that are sweeping the globe. This discourse must set itself the task of reflexively linking the elements of these changes with the goal of building an inclusive society, based on the principles of common citizenship. The extent of a common citizenship, based on access to social, political and civil rights, will be the ultimate test of the depth of Irish civil society.

Appendix 1: Methodology of Research

Objectives of research

The objective of the empirical research was to generate a variety of data sources from which a multi-layered framework for assessing the relationship between civil society and the voluntary sector could be derived. A complex research strategy was devised, which had three arms:

1. A national population survey, which identified attitudes towards the voluntary sector and the strength of communitarian values in Irish society. The survey focused on issues such as the level of involvement with the voluntary sector, attitudes towards the voluntary sector as an efficient provider of social services and the level of commitment to principles of social trust and moral obligation. (See Appendix 2 for questionnaire used in the national population survey.)

2. A survey of voluntary organisations by postal questionnaire, which focused on providing information on the changing reality of the civic environment as experienced by voluntary organisations. The questionnaire explored issues faced by voluntary organisations such as funding, volunteer recruitment and involvement with the State. (See Appendix 3 for both the questionnaire used in the survey and Appendix 4 for the list of voluntary organisations that took part.)

3. Face-to-face interviews with representatives of a variety of voluntary organisations, which provided an opportunity for more extensive exploration of the issues affecting the contribution of the voluntary sector to the definition of civil society in Ireland. (See Appendix 4 for the list of voluntary organisations interviewed.)

Implementation of research

1. National population survey

The survey took the form of participation in the Taylor Nelson AGB Omnibus survey for the period 25 June to 23 July, 1996. A total of 1020 interviews were achieved with adults aged 15+ years. All interviewing was carried out face-to-face with respondents in their own homes. As part of the Omnibus survey a total of 60 sampling points were selected throughout the Republic of Ireland. At each sample point, 17 respondents were interviewed. The weights of the Omnibus survey are weighted to reflect the population parameters of adults in the Republic of Ireland. The data for the setting of quotas are derived from the 1991 Census of Population produced by the Central Statistics Office, Ireland.

2. Survey of voluntary organisations

As part of the preliminary phase of the design of the research tool, a pilot questionnaire was sent to five organisations. The results of the pilot survey contributed to the design of the final questionnaire. During spring 1996, a postal questionnaire was sent to voluntary organisations listed in the 1994–1995 National Social Service Board Directory of Voluntary Organisations. This Directory was chosen because it contained a broad range of different types of organisations working across a wide variety of fields. In total 579 questionnaires

178

were sent out of which 261 were returned, which gives a total response rate of 45%.

The 248 returned questionnaires were broken down as follows:

- 13 were not completed – the relevant organisation stated that it did not feel it belonged to the category of voluntary organisation
- 12 organisations did not complete the questionnaire but enclosed documentation that they felt may be relevant
- 8 questionnaires were returned marked 'gone away' or 'unknown'
- 2 organisations returned uncompleted questionnaires stating that they did not have the staff or sufficient funding to spend time on it
- 2 questionnaires were returned uncompleted as the organisation had disbanded
- 1 organisation returned an uncompleted questionnaire as its Head Office was going to complete it for all the branches
- 223 organisations returned completed questionnaires.

3. Interviews with representatives of voluntary organisations

Interviews took place with representatives of 16 voluntary organisations from November 1996 to January 1997. Interviews were based on an open-question format. Interviewees were invited to discuss a number of issues facing the voluntary sector, such as relationships with the statutory sector, funding requirements, recruitment of volunteers and degree of account-ability and democracy within their organisational structures. The interviews provided an extended opportunity to explore some of the findings raised in the other phases of the research. Organisations were selected for interview on the basis of their involvement across a number of fields of social service provision. This provided a comparative aspect in the assessment of the linkages between the relevant issues facing the voluntary sector and the broader concept of civil society.

<u>Voluntary Organisation Section</u>

I would now like to talk to you about **Voluntary Organisations**. By voluntary organisation I mean:

voluntary organisations/charities providing social services, welfare service, health services

or

voluntary organisations/charities providing cultural, sporting or leisure activities

or

political organisations, trade unions or professional associations.

Q.1 Have you ever had involvement with a voluntary organisation in any of the following ways?

Read out and rotate order between interviews.

Tick Start		Yes	No
	Paid employee of a voluntary organisation.	1	2
	Employed by a voluntary organisation as part of a government employment scheme.	1	2
	Given your services without pay to a voluntary organisation (i.e. a volunteer either because you were a member of the organisation or just an interested member of the general public).	1	2

Q.2 Show card V1.

When you think of moral issues in Ireland such as divorce, single-parents, abortion, homosexuality, etc., please choose one of the following statements to best describe your attitude:(Single code only)

I think we have become too liberal and I wish Ireland was more like it was in the past.	1
I think we have the right balance at the moment.	2
I think we need to go further and be more liberal.	3

Q.3 Show card V2.

I am going to read out a series of statements some people have made about Voluntary Organisations. For each statement I read out, can you tell to what extent you agree or disagree, using one of the statements on this card.

Read out and rotate order between interviews.

	Agree strongly	Agree slightly	Disagree slightly	Disagree strongly	Don't know	OUO
Voluntary organisations usually deal with the people who use their services in a fair, open and honest way.	1	2	4	5	6	7
Voluntary organisations have a poor record in solving the problems of the people they try to help.	1	2	4	5	6	7
I feel morally obliged to donate money to voluntary organisations.	1	2	4	5	6	7
I am fed up with voluntary organisations always asking me for donations.	1	2	4	5	6	7
I believe that it is better for voluntary organisations to look after vulnerable members of society rather than the State looking after them.	1	2	4	5	6	7
If the government asked me to pay more tax I would prefer the money was spent on improving the welfare services provided by the State, rather than the State passing it to voluntary organisations for them to provide the welfare services.	1	2	4	5	6	7

	Agree strongly	Agree slightly	Disagree slightly	Disagree strongly	Don't know	OUO
I would like the people in the local community where I live to be more involved with each other.	1	2	4	5	6	7
To survive in this life you must grab what you can and not worry about other members of society too much.	1	2	4	5	6	7
Ireland is still a fairly united society because most people hold the same values when it comes to important matters	1	2	4	5	6	7

Q.4   Are you currently giving your services as a volunteer to a voluntary organisation?

Yes	1
No	2

If 'no' at Q.4 ask Q.5.

Q.5   Show card V2 again.

Again, can you tell me to what extent you agree or disagree with the statements on this card.

Read out.

	Agree strongly	Agree slightly	Disagree slightly	Disagree strongly	Don't know	OUO
I do not want to give up some of my spare time to do voluntary work.	1	2	4	5	6	7
I would like to give up some of my spare time to do voluntary work if my circumstances allowed it.	1	2	4	5	6	7

Part One — General information.

1. The questionnaire is being completed by many different types of organisations, ranging from large national head offices to small local branches. Please tick **one** description in the table below to show which type of organisation you are completing the questionnaire as, and answer the rest of the questionnaire in relation to the answer you have ticked here.

National voluntary organisation mainly operating from this one centre/branch.

Local voluntary group mainly operating from this one centre/branch.

National voluntary organisation with affiliated local branches /groups /services / member organisations, etc., with within or outside the Republic of Ireland.

Local voluntary organisation with affiliated local branches /groups /services / member organisations, etc.

National voluntary organisation working with non-affiliated groups/organisations either within or outside the Republic of Ireland.

Local voluntary organisation working with non-affiliated groups/organisations locally.

Other (please describe).

2a. Does the work of your organisation involve contact with Northern Ireland in any way?

2b. If yes, please describe.

3. In what year was your organisation first formed?

Part Two — Comparing when your organisation was first formed to now.

4. When your organisation was **first formed** what was its **main** role and what **other** roles did it aim to perform?

Main role — tick **one** only. Other roles — tick **as many** as you wish.

Role of organisation when first formed:

Umbrella organisation.

Providing services (i.e. social, health or welfare provision to particular client/user groups, including the provision of counselling and support services).

Promoting self-help or mutual aid.

Promoting local community involvement or neighbourhood organisations.

Providing information (to client, user, professionals, government, etc.).

Providing education or training (to client, user, professionals, etc.).

Promoting a cause (e.g., feminism, environmentalism, peace, human rights, civil rights, etc.), campaigning, lobbying or pressure group.

Promoting research (either by carrying it out or funding/fund-raising for research).

Cultural/hobby group.

Other (please describe).

5. When your organisation was **first formed** which of the following statements were applicable? Tick **as many** as you wish.

183

The organisation was set up to meet a need which was not being met by any other organisation, either statutory or voluntary.

Other voluntary organisations were carrying out similar work but not meeting need sufficiently.

Statutory organisations were carrying out similar work but not meeting need sufficiently.

Other voluntary organisations were already adequately meeting need and we aimed to supplement their work.

Statutory organisations were already adequately meeting need and we aimed to supplement their work.

6. Referring to your organisation as it operates now, what is its main role and what other roles does it aim to perform? Main role—tick one only. Other roles—tick as many as you wish.

Role of organisation now:

Umbrella organisation.

Providing services (i.e. social, health or welfare provision to particular client/user groups, including the provision of counselling and support services).

Promoting self-help or mutual aid.

Promoting local community involvement or neighbourhood organisations.

Providing information (to client, user, professionals, government, etc.).

Providing education or training (to client, user, professionals, etc.).

Promoting a cause (e.g., feminism, environmentalism, peace, human rights, civil rights, etc.), campaigning, lobbying or pressure group.

Promoting research (either by carrying it out or funding/fund-raising for research).

Cultural/hobby group.

Other (please describe).

7. Referring to your organisation as it operates now, which of the following statements are applicable? Tick as many as you wish.

The organisation is meeting a need which is not being met by any other organisation, either statutory or voluntary.

Other voluntary organisations are carrying out similar work but not meeting need sufficiently.

Statutory organisations are carrying out similar work but not meeting need sufficiently.

Other voluntary organisations are already adequately meeting need and we aim to supplement their work.

Statutory organisations are already adequately meeting need and we aim to supplement their work.

Part Three—Changes which have affected your organisation over the past few years

Note: For those organisations formed before 1976, please complete the following section by comparing 1975 to 1995. For those organisations formed in 1976 or later, please complete the following section by comparing the year your organisation was formed to 1995.

184

8a. Please indicate whether your organisation did in the past, and does now, target specific groups of people to work with. Tick as many as you like for each year (in 1975, or year organisation formed if after 1975; in 1995).

Note: If your organisation does not target specific groups but works with the whole community, go to question 9.

Specific groups of people organisation did and does target:

Children.

Young people.

The elderly.

Women.

Families.

Gay and lesbian people.

People with a specific illness, e.g. cancer (please specify).

People with a specific need, e.g. bereavement counselling (please specify).

People with a physical disability.

People with a mental handicap/learning disability/learning difficulty.

People with a mental health problem.

People with a drug abuse problem.

People with an alcohol abuse problem.

People who are unemployed.

People who are homeless.

People with a housing concern.

People living in particular geographical locations (please specify).

The travelling community.

Carers.

Non-Irish people living in Ireland.

Non-Irish people living outside of Ireland.

Other (please specify).

8b. Please add any comments you wish about your answer to question 9a concerning any changes in the groups of people targeted.

9. Please indicate the **approximate** percentage of your income derived from the following sources in the past and now. (In 1975, or year organisation formed if after 1975; in 1995.)

Percentage of income derived from:

European funding.

Statutory funding.

Funding from non-statutory groups. Please specify, e.g. commercial /religious / charitable/other voluntary organisation/trust funds, etc.

Funding from National Lottery.

Membership fees.

Charges for services.

Organised fund-raising events/activities.

Individual personal giving/donations.

Other.

10a. Has the introduction of the National Lottery affected the overall financial position of your organisation? Please tick **one only**.

Yes, in a positive way.

Yes, in a negative way.

No.

10b. Please explain your answer to question 10a.

11a. Please compare the past (i.e., either 1975, or the year your organisation was formed if after 1975) and tick **one** of the following statements concerning voluntary donations from the general public (either at fund-raising events or through individual giving):

Our organisation finds it **more difficult** to raise money in this way now when compared to the past.

Our organisation finds **no change** in raising money in this way now when compared to the past.

Our organisation finds it **easier** to raise money in this way now when compared to the past.

11b. If your answer to question 11a is **easier** or **more difficult**, please explain why you think this is so.

12. Please fill in **approximate** numbers below (where applicable). (1975, or year organisation formed if after 1975; 1995.)

Number of paid staff — full-time.

Number of paid staff — part-time.

Numbers of staff on employment schemes.

Number of volunteers.

Number of members.

Number of clients/users of your services in the year.

13a. Please compare the past (i.e. either 1975, or the year your organisation was formed if after 1975) and tick **one** of the following statements concerning the services of volunteers.

Our organisation finds it **easier** to recruit the services of volunteers now when compared to the past.

Our organisation finds **no change** in recruiting the services of volunteers now when compared to the past.

Our organisation finds it **more difficult** to recruit the services of volunteers now when compared to the past.

13b. If your answer to question 14a is either **easier** or **more difficult**, please explain why you think this is so.

14a. Please compare the past (i.e., either 1975, or the year your organisation was formed if after 1975) and tick **one** of the following statements concerning the ability of your organisation to meet the needs of your clients, users or members.

Our organisation finds it **more difficult** to meet the needs of our clients/users/members now when compared to the past.

Our organisation finds **no change** in meeting the needs of our clients/users/members now

186

when compared to the past.

Our organisation finds it **easier** to meet the needs of our clients/user/members now when compared to the past.

14b. If your answer to question 14a is either **easier** or **more difficult**, please explain why you think this is so.

15a. Please compare the past (i.e. either 1975, or the year your organisation was formed if after 1975) and tick either—**more, less, same,** or **neither** for (a) to (e) in the table below.

The organisation promotes the ethos of self-help/mutual aid amongst our clients/users/members.

The organisation works to empower our clients/users/members.

The organisation is concerned with equal opportunities to encourage particular groups to use our services.

The organisation works with local community groups.

The organisation works in democratic way.

15b. If your answer to question 15a is either **more** or **less** please explain:

Self-help/mutual aid.

Empowerment.

Equal opportunities.

Working with local communities.

Democracy within the organisation.

16. Referring to your organisation as it operates now, please tick either: a **lot/some/a little** or **none** for (a) to (c) in the table below. The amount of influence volunteers have over decisions-making within our organisation is.

The amount of influence clients/users/members have over decision-making within our organisation is.

The amount of power our organisation has in relation to the decision-making policies of relevant statutory organisations (i.e. local authority/health board/statutory body/ government) is.

17. Referring the work your organisation is involved in now, please tick whether you think the State should have either: **more, less,** or **about the same** involvement for (a) to (e) in the table below.

Providing the services itself.

Providing funding for the organisation.

Monitoring the performance of the organisation.

Enforcing standards in the organisation.

Training volunteers or staff in the organisation.

18. Referring to the work your organisation is involved in now, please tick either: **strongly agree, agree, disagree,** or **strongly disagree** for (a) to (k) in the table below (where applicable).

Co-ordination and communication with other voluntary organisations working in the same field is inadequate.

187

Co-ordination and communication with State bodies working in the same field is adequate.

Our organisation is not adequately accountable to its funding bodies.

Our organisation is adequately accountable to its clients/users/members.

Irish people are not generally very supportive of our organisation in terms of financial donations.

19. What would you say is the **main** change which has occurred in your organisation since 1975, or the year the organisation was formed if after 1975?

20. What would you pick as the **main** thing your organisation is doing successfully at the moment?

Thank you for your co-operation

Appendix 4: Organisations that Returned Postal Questionnaire and that Provided Representatives to be Interviewed

Organisations that returned postal questionnaires

Action for Mobility

Adoptive Parents Association of Ireland

Age Action Ireland, Ltd

AIDS Help West

Amputee Support Association

L'Arche Communities

Association for Children and Adults with Learning Disabilities (Dyslexia Association)

Association for Retired Insurance Staff

Bereavement Counselling Service

Body Positive

CADDD (Campaign Against Dangerous and Drunken Driving)

Cairde

Camphill Village Community (Kilkenny)

CAN — Community Action Network

Care for Dublin's Old Folk Living Alone

Carmichael Centre for Voluntary Groups

Catholic Guides of Ireland

Centre for Independent Living, The

Cerebral Palsy Ireland (Limerick)

Child Minders' Union

Civil Defence

Cleft Lip and Palate Association of Ireland

Comhaltas Ceoltóirí Éireann

Comhlámh

Confederation of Peace Corps

Conservation Volunteers Ireland

Co-operation North

Cork AIDS Alliance

Daddy (Drinking and Driving Don't Yield)

Adapt

AFRI (Action from Ireland)

Age and Opportunity

Aim Group Family Law Information, Mediation and Counselling Centre

Anklosing Spondylitis Association of Ireland

Arthritis Foundation of Ireland

Association for the Psychiatric Study of Adolescents

Association of Occupational Therapists of Ireland (AOTI)

Between

The Brabazon Trust

CAFÉ (Creative Activity for Everyone)

Camphill Village Community (Monaghan)

Camphill Village Community (Tipperary)

Canteen Ireland

Carers Association

Catholic Boy Scouts of Ireland/Gasóga Catóilicí na hÉireann

Catholic Marriage Advisory Council

Cerebral Palsy Ireland (Cork)

Cherish

Children's Leukaemia Research Project

Clanwilliam Institute

Coeliac Society of Ireland

Comhdháil Náisiúnta na Gaeilge

Community Welfare Officers' Association

Conflict Resolution Services

Consumers' Association of Ireland

Co-operative Development Society

Council for the Status of Women

Disability Federation of Ireland

Divorce Action Group

Dublin Council for the Aged

Dublin Society for Prevention of Cruelty
to Animals, Inc.

ECO—The Irish Environmental
Conservation Organisation for
Youth—UNESCO Clubs

Educate Together

Environmental Health Officers'
Association

Family Law Action Group

Federation of Active Retirement
Associations

Film Institute of Ireland

Focus Housing Association

Friedreich's Ataxia Society Ireland

Genesis

Headway Ireland (National Head
Injuries Association)

Higher Education for Development Co-
operation (HEDCO)

Housing Association for Integrated
Living

Hyperactive Children's Support Group,
Ireland

Impero (Irish Mental Patients
Educational and Representative
Organisation)

Innisfree Housing Association

Interculture Ireland

Irish American Parnership

Irish Association for Cultural, Economic
and Social Relations

Irish Association for Spina Bifida and
Hydrocephalus

Irish Association of Social Workers

Irish Cancer Society

Irish Council against Blood Sports

Irish Council for Social Housing

Irish Family Heart Association

Irish Foster Care Association

The Irish Girl Guides

The Down's Syndrome Association of
Ireland

Dublin Road Safety Council

Dublin Youth Theatre

Edel House

Energy Action Limited

Experiment in International Living

Feachtas—Óg Gluaiseacht na Gaeilge

Federation of Services for Unmarried
Parents and their Children

Financial Information Service Centres

Forum of People with Disabilities

Friends of the Suicide Bereaved

Hanly Centre, The

Helpful Hands

Home Birth Centre of Ireland

Huntington's Disease Association

Ileostomy and Colostomy Association
Southern Ireland Division

Inland Waterways Association of Ireland

Interaid

Ireland Funds, The

Irish ANTS Co., Ltd (Syringomyelia Self-
Help Group)

Irish Association for Gifted Children/An
Óige Thréitheach

Irish Association of Care Workers

Irish Astronomical Society

Irish Childbirth Trust

Irish Council for Civil Liberties

Irish Family History Society

Irish Family Planning Association

Irish Foundation for Co-operative
Development, Ltd.

Irish Guide Dogs Association

190

Irish Hard of Hearing Association
Irish League of Credit Unions
Irish ME Trust
Irish Motor Neurone Disease
  Association
Irish Naturist Association
Irish Peatland Conservation Council
Irish Raynaud's and Scleroderma
  Society
Irish Society for Autism

Irish Society for the Prevention of
  Cruelty to Children
Irish Sudden Infant Death Association
Irish Wildlife Federation
Le Chéile
Lesbian and Gay Resource Group
Life Pregnancy Care Service (Cork)
London Irish Centre — Community
  Services Dept
Los Angeles Society
Marriage Counselling Services Ltd.
Mediators Institute Ireland
MS Ireland (The Multiple Sclerosis
  Society of Ireland)
National Adult Literacy Agency

National Association for Victims of
  Bullying
National Association of Tenants'
  Organisations (for tenants and
  residents)
National Council for the Blind of Ireland
National Eczema Society
National Federation of Pensioners'
  Associations
National Irish Safety Organisation
National Youth Council of Ireland
Óige, An (Irish Youth Hostel
  Association)
PACE (Prisoners Aid through
  Community Effort)
Parentline
People's College for Continuing
  Education and Training

Irish International Peace Movement
Irish Lupus Support Group Ltd
Irish Missionary Union, The
Irish National Organisation of the
  Unemployed
Irish Peace Institute
Irish Pre-School Playgroups Association
Irish Red Cross Society

Irish Society for Colitis and Crohn's
  Disease
Irish Stillbirth and Neonatal Death Society

Irish Traveller Movement
Irish Youth Foundation
Leprosy Mission of Ireland, The
Life Pregnancy Care Service (Dublin)
Liffey Trust Ltd, The
London Irish Women's Centre

Maritime Institute of Ireland
Marrowbone Lane Fund
Mothers' Union
Myasthenia Gravis Association

National Association for the Mentally
  Handicapped of Ireland (NAMHI)
National Association for Youth Drama
  (NAYD)
National Association of Widows in
  Ireland

National Council of YMCAs of Ireland Ltd
National Federation of Arch Clubs
National Grave Association (Cumann na
  nUaigheann Náisiúnta)
National Parents Council — Primary
Neurofibromatosis Association (Phone)
Order of Malta and Order of Malta
  Ambulance Corps
Parental Equality

Peacehaven Trust
Pioneer Total Abstinence Association of
  the Sacred Heart

An Post Retired Officials Association
Psychological Society of Ireland (PSI)
Reach
Refugee Agency
Rehabilitation Institute (Offaly)
Retirement Planning Council

Royal British Legion (Republic of
Ireland Area) and Royal British Legion
Women's Section, The
Rubinstein-Taybi Syndrome Support
Group
The Samaritans (Dublin)
Schizophrenia Association of Ireland
SHARE (Schoolboys Harness Aid for
Relief of Elderly)
Society for the Protection of Unborn
Children Ireland Ltd
SOFT—Support Organisation for
Trisomy 13/18
Soroptimist International—Republic of
Ireland—National Project 'Caring for
the Carers'
STEPS Youth Advice and Counselling
Service (Cork)
Threshold
Transvestite Line
Trust for Community Initiatives
Voluntary Service International (VSI)
Volunteer Stroke Scheme (Waterford)
Volunteer Stroke Scheme (Mayo)
Women's Aid

Protestant Aid
Rape Crisis Centre
Recovery, Inc.
Rehabilitation Institute (Cavan)
Rehabilitation Institute (Dublin)
Riding for the Disabled Association
Ireland
Royal National Lifeboat Institution

Rural Resettlement Ireland Ltd

The Samaritans (Waterford)
Self Help Development International
Simon Community

Society of St Vincent de Paul

Soldiers', Sailors' and Airmen's Families
Association/Help Society
Spinal Injuries Action Association

Swim

Toy Library Group Ireland
Trust
Vegetarian Society of Ireland
Volunteer Stroke Scheme (Dublin)
Volunteer Stroke Scheme (Kildare)
Waterford Drug Abuse Resource Group
Women's Political Association (WPA)

Organisations that provided representatives to be interviewed

Community Action Network
Cork Association for the Deaf
Crosscare
Dublin Rape Crisis Centre

Focus Point

National Association for Mental
Handicap in Ireland
Ogra Chorcai
Travellers Visibility Group (Cork)

Cork Aids Alliance
Cork Threshold
Disability Federation of Ireland
Edel House (hostel for homeless women in
Cork)
Irish Society for the Prevention of Cruelty to
Children (Cork)
National Youth Federation

Samaritans
Victim Support

Appendix 5: Outstanding Tables of Data for Chapter 5

Table 1. Percentage of population that would be in favour, if the Government asked them, to pay more tax and would prefer if the money was spent on improving the welfare services provided by the State, rather than being passed to voluntary organisations for them to provide the welfare services

	% of general pop.	% of pop. who have had involvement with voluntary organisations	% of pop. who have had no involvement with voluntary organisations
agree	42	47	38
disagree	31	33	30

Table 2. Percentage of population that believe that the following Statement reflects their attitudes towards issues such as divorce, single parents, abortion, homosexuality, etc.

	% of general pop.	% of pop. who have had involvement with voluntary organisations	% of pop. who have had no involvement with voluntary organisations
Ireland has become too liberal and wish Ireland was more like it was in the past	40	41	39
Ireland has the right balance at the moment	31	30	31
Ireland needs to be more liberal	27	25	28
Other	1	2	1
None	1	2	1

Table 3. Client groups of organisations in past and in present

Client groups	In 1975, or year organisation was formed if after 1975		In 1995	
	N	%	N	%
Children	36	17%	52	24%
Young people	52	24%	67	31%
The Elderly	36	17%	39	18%
Women	38	17%	52	24%
Families	47	22%	54	25%
Gay or lesbian people	8	4%	14	7%
People with a specific illness	40	18%	42	19%
People with a specific need	50	23%	54	25%
People with a physical disability	33	15%	43	20%
People with a mental handicap/ learning disability/difficulty	25	12%	27	13%
People with a mental health problem	15	7%	20	9%
People with a drug abuse problem	7	3%	14	7%
People with an alcohol abuse problem	10	4%	11	5%
People who are unemployed	22	10%	30	14%
People who are homeless	20	9%	21	10%
People with a housing concern	21	9%	26	12%
People living in particular geographical locations	16	7%	26	12%
Travelling community	10	4%	16	7%
Carers	22	10%	28	13%
Non-Irish people living in Ireland	5	2%	7	3%
Non-Irish people living outside Ireland	8	4%	9	4%
Other	52	24%	63	29%

Valid cases 215–219

Appendix 6: Outstanding Tables of Data for Chapter 6

Table 1. Breakdown of population who gave their services without pay to a voluntary organisation

		(Percentage of each category giving service)
Gender (%)	men	31
	women	33
Social class (%)	ABC1	43
	C2DE	25
	Farm	34
Region (%)	Dub	33
	Len	47
	Mun	24
	Con/Uls	24
Location (%)	Rural	33
	Urban	34
Married/ single (%)	Married	36
	Single	28
Presence of children (%)	None	30
	6–14 yrs	34
	less 5 yrs	29

Table 2. Age profile of population who who gave their services without pay to a voluntary organisation

	15–34 years (%)	35–54 years (%)	55+ years (%)
Age profile of total population	42	32	26
Age profile of total population who volunteered	27	42	25

Table 3. Breakdown of population who are currently giving their services to a voluntary organisation

		(Percentage of each category giving service)
Gender (%)	men	17
	women	19
Social class (%)	ABC1	24
	C2DE	14
	Farm	22
Region (%)	Dubl	13
	Lens	25
	Mun	17
	Conn/Uls	18
Location (%)	Rural	22
	Urban	20
Age group (%)	15–34 yrs	14
	35–54 yrs	26
	55+ years	15

Table 4. Breakdown of population who are not currently giving their services to a voluntary organisation and willingness/unwillingness to use their spare time for voluntary work.

		Don't Know	Willing	Unwilling
Gender (%)	men	17	57	26
	women	9	73	18
Social class (%)	ABC1	9	74	17
	C2DE	13	63	24
	Far	19	55	26
Region (%)	Dubl	16	69	15
	Len	5	74	21
	Mun	14	61	25
	Con/Uls	13	57	30
Location (%)	Rural	15	60	25
	Urban	5	72	23
Age group (%)	15-34 yrs	13	54	30
	35-54 yrs	11	69	20
	55+ years	16	69	18

Table 5. Numbers of staff, clients, members, etc. of organisations in 1975 (or year of formation if after 1975) and 1995

	Year	No. of staff, clients, members and volunteers					
		0	1–10	11–50	51–200	201–500	500+
(i) Paid staff/full	1975	121	57	9	1	0	0
-time	1995	93	85	26	5	0	0
(ii) Paid staff/part	1975	158	30	1	0	0	0
-time	1995	115	84	5	5	0	0
(iii) Staff on employment	1975	181	7	1	0	0	0
schemes	1995	142	43	18	4	1	0
(iv) Volunteers	1975	42	66	35	13	1	15
	1995	44	48	55	22	9	21
(v) Members	1975	50	20	35	32	13	23
	1995	49	7	29	33	28	54
(vi) Clients/	1975	5	17	23	20	16	18
users of service	1995	0	3	15	36	17	73

Appendix 7: Outstanding Table of Data for Chapter 7

Table 1. *Comments of organisations on effect of National Lottery*

Comments	Number of organisations	% of responses
Positive effect because it has provided a new source of funds	29	20%
Positive effect because received funds are easier than fund-raising from general public	2	1%
Positive effect because received funds are easier than fund-raising from other statutory sources	2	1%
Negative effect because organisation has experienced a drop in other forms of fund-raising	27	19%
Negative effect on general fund-raising because public believe that National Lottery money goes to charitable organisations	2	1%
No effect because never applied	8	6%
No effect because never applied – did not believe they would qualify	29	20%
Very little effect because only ever received very small amount	2	1%
No effect because fund-raising is not of that type	29	20%
No effect because government funding has been replaced by National Lottery funding	6	4%
Other	6	4%

Valid cases 144   Missing cases 79

Bibliography

Advisory Group on Charities/Fund-raising Legislation (1996) *Report of The Advisory Group on Charities/Fundraising Legislation*, Department of Justice, Dublin.

Anderson, D. (1996) Bringing Civil Society to an Uncivilised Place, in C. Haunt, E. Dunne, *Civil Society*, Routledge, London.

Anheier, H. and Salamon, L. (1994) Caring Sector or Caring Society? Discovering the Non-profit Sector Cross-Nationally, *Working Paper No. 17*, The Johns Hopkins University Institute for Policy Studies, Baltimore, MD.

Beck, U. (1997) *The Reinvention of Politics*, Polity, Oxford.

Beck, U., Giddens, A. and Lash, S. (1994) *Reflexive Modernisation*, Polity, Oxford.

Berking, H. (1996) Solidary Individualism, in Lash, S., Szerszynski, B. and Wynne, B. (eds), *Risk, Environment, & Modernity*, Sage, London.

Billis, D. (1993) *Organising Public and Voluntary Agencies*, Routledge, London.

Borrie Report (1994) *Commission on Social Justice*, Viking Press, London.

Bradshaw, B. (1974) *The Dissolution of the Religious Orders in Ireland Under Henry VIII*, Cambridge University Press, Cambridge.

Brady, J. (1976) The Law on Charity, *Northern Ireland Legal Quarterly*, 27, 3.

Breen, R., Hannan, D., Rottman, D. and Whelan, C. (1990) *Understanding Contemporary Ireland: State, Class and Development in the Republic of Ireland*, Gill & Macmillan, Dublin.

Brenton, M. (1985) *The Voluntary Sector in British Social Services*, Longman, London.

Brindle, D. (1997) Charities worried as fewer people make donations, *The Guardian*, 30 June.

Bruce, M. (1968) *The Coming of the Welfare State*, Batsford, London.

Bulmer, M. (1986) *The Social Basis of Community Care*, Allen & Unwin, London.

Butler, F. (1981) Voluntary Inaction, *Community Care*, 19 February.

Carmen, R. (1990) *Communication, Education & Empowerment*, University of

Manchester, Manchester.

Catholic Directory, (1836) Dublin.

Cohen, J. & Arato, A. (1992) *Civil Society and Political Theory*, MIT Press, Cambridge, MA.

Cohen, R. (1995) Capitalism Brings Rich Pickings, *Washington Post/Guardian Weekly*, 30 April.

Cole, G. D. H. and Postgate, R. (1961) *The Common People*, Methuen, London.

Combat Poverty Agency (1988) *Poverty and the Social Welfare System*, ESRI, Dublin.

Combat Poverty Agency (1996) *Poverty in the 1990s*, Combat Poverty/ESRI, Dublin.

Commission of European Communities (1993) *Green Paper*, European Social Policy—Options for Union, Com (93) 55 1.

Connolly, J. (1956) *Labour in Irish History*, New Books Publications, Dublin.

Cork Community Development Institute Archives.

Costello Report—Committee on Fund-raising Activities for Charitable and Other Purposes (1990) Stationery Office, Dublin.

Council for Social Welfare (1991) *Submission to White Paper on the Voluntary Sector*, Council for Social Welfare, Dublin.

Cousins, M. (1994) *A Guide to Legal Structures for Voluntary and Community Organisations* Combat Poverty Agency, Dublin.

Cousins, P. (1978) Participation and Pluralism in South London, *London Journal*, No. 42.

Crickley, A. and Devlin, M. (1990) In *Community Work in Ireland: Trends in the 80's, Options for the 90's*, Combat Poverty Agency, Dublin.

Croft, S. and Beresford, P. (1986) Whose Welfare: *Private Care or Private Welfare*, Russell Press, Brighton.

Crowley, N. (1993) Racism and Travellers, in DTEG/ICCL/ITM *Anti-Racism Law and the Travellers*, ITM, Dublin.

Culpitt, I. (1992) *Welfare and Citizenship: Beyond the Crisis of the Welfare State*, Sage, London.

Curry, J. (1980) *The Irish Social Services*, Institute of Public Administration, Dublin.

Curry, J. (1982) *The Development of Voluntary Social Services in Ireland*, National Social Services Board, Dublin.

Curtis, J. (1971) *American Sociological Review*, Vol. 36, October, Columbus, Ohio.

Dahl, R. (1971) *Polyarchy: Participation and Opposition*, Yale University

Press, New Haven, CT.

Dahrendorf, R. (1994) The Changing Quality of Citizenship, in B. van Steenbergen (ed.), *The Condition of Citizenship*, Sage, London.

Darvil, G. and Mundy, B. (1984) *Volunteers in the Personal Social Services*, Tavistock, London.

Davis, E. E. *et al.* (1984) *Attitudes towards Poverty and Related Social Issues in Ireland*, ESRI Paper No. 117, Dublin.

Davis-Smith, J. In Billis, D. And Harris, M. (1996) *Voluntary Agencies: Challenges of Organisation and Management*, Macmillan, London.

De Swann, A. (1988) *In Care of the State: Health, Education, and Welfare in Europe*, Polity, Cambridge.

De Tocqueville, A. (1956) *Democracy in America* (ed. R. D. Heffner), Mentor, New York.

Dean, M. (1991) *The Constitution of Poverty*, Routledge, London.

Department of Enterprise and Employment (1997) *Press Release*, February, Dublin.

Department of Social Welfare (1997) *Supporting Voluntary Activity: A Green Paper on the Community and Voluntary Sector and its Relationship with the State*, Stationery Office, Dublin.

Department of the Environment (1996) *Better Local Government: A Programme for Change*, Government Publications, Dublin.

Department of Health (1966) *Care of the Aged Report*, Government Publications, Dublin.

Department of Health (1988) *The Years Ahead: A Policy for the Elderly*, Government Publications, Dublin.

Department of Social Welfare (1997) *Sharing in Progress: National Anti-Poverty Strategy*, Stationery Office, Dublin.

Dobbs, A. (1729) *An Essay on Trade & Improvement in Ireland*, Dublin.

Donoghue, F. and Ruddle, H. (1995) *The Organisation of Volunteering: A Study of Irish Voluntary Organisations in the Social Welfare Area*, Policy Research Centre, National College of Industrial Relations, Dublin.

Donzelot, J. (1980) *The Policing of Families*, Hutchinson, London.

Elias, N. (1939) *The Civilising Process : The History of Manners*, Blackwell, Oxford.

Esping-Andersen, G. (1990) *The Three Worlds of Welfare Capitalism*, Polity Press, Cambridge.

Etzioni, A. (1994), *The Spirit of Community*, Touchstone, New York.

European Union (1996) *Report by the Comité des Sagés for a Europe of Civil and*

Social Rights, European Commission, Luxembourg.

Faughnan, P. (1990) *Partners in Progress: The Role of NGO's in the Social Services*, Dept. of Social Welfare, Dublin.

Faughnan, P. and Kelleher, P. (1993) *The Voluntary Sector and the State*, CMRS, Dublin.

Forde, C. (1996) History of Community Work, in P. Burgess (ed.), *Youth & Community Work*, UCC, Cork.

Fraser, D. (1973) *The Evolution of the British Welfare State*, London, Macmillan.

Fukuyama, F. (1995) *Trust: The Social Virtues and the Creation of Prosperity*, London, Hamish Hamilton.

Gans, H. (1996) From Underclass to Undercaste, in E. Mingione, *Urban Poverty and the Underclass*, Blackwell, Oxford.

Gaskin, K. and Smith, J. (1995) *A New Civic Europe? A Study of the Extent and Role of Volunteering*, Volunteer Centre, London.

Gellner, E. (1994) *Conditions of Liberty: Civil Society and Its Rivals*, Hamish Hamilton, London.

Gerard, D. (1985) What makes a volunteer? *New Society*, 8 November.

Giddens, A. (1994) *Beyond Left and Right: The Future of Radical Politics*, Polity Press, Cambridge.

Giddens, A. (1991) *Modernity and Self Identity*, Polity, Oxford.

Gilder, G. (1981) *Wealth and Poverty*, Bantam Books, London.

Gladstone, F.J. (1979) *Voluntary Action in a Changing World*, Bedford Square Press, London.

Goodin, R. (1988) *Reasons for Welfare*, Princetown University Press, Princetown NJ.

Gorz, A. (1982) *Farewell to the Working Class*, London.

Gramsci, A. (1971) *Selection from Prison Notebooks* (eds Q. Hoare & G. Howell Smith), London.

Habermas, J. (1987) *The Theory of Communicative Action*, Vol. 2, Polity, Oxford.

Handy, C. (1988) *Understanding Voluntary Organisations*, Penguin, London.

Hann, C. and Dunn, E. (eds) (1996) *Civil Society: Challenging Western Models*, Routledge, London.

Harvey, B. (1993) *The Prospects for an Umbrella Organisation for the Voluntary Sector in Ireland*, The Enterprise Trust, Dublin.

Harvey, B. (1995) *The National Lottery: Ten Years On*, Policy Research Centre, NCIR, Dublin.

Hatch, S. (1980) *Outside the State: Voluntary Organisations in Three Towns*, Croom Helm, London.

Havel, V. (1993) The Post Communist Nightmare, *New York Review of Books*, 27 May.

Hayek, F. (1976) *The Mirage of Social Justice*, Routledge & Kegan Paul, London.

Healy, S. (1990) *Must the Poor Always Wait?* Dublin, CMRS.

Hedley, R. and Smith, J.D. (1992) *Volunteering and Society: Principles and Practice*, NCVO, London.

Hoggett, P. (1994) *The Future of Civic Forms of Organisation*, Demos, London.

Ignatieff, M. (1997) Problems of Erasing Humiliation in a Decent Society, *Times Literary Supplement*, 7 March.

Inglis, H.D. (1835) *Ireland in 1834*, London.

Ireland (1987) *The Programme for National Recovery*, Government Publications, Dublin.

Ireland (1990) *Programme for Economic and Social Progress*, Government Publications, Dublin.

Ireland (1994) *Programme for Competiveness and Work*, Government Publications, Dublin.

Ireland (1997) *Programme 2000*, Government Publications, Dublin.

Irish Council for Social Housing (1991) *Newsletter*, No. 33, Dublin.

Irish Times (1992) Address by President Mary Robinson to Dáil Eireann, Dublin, 9 July.

Jaffro, G. (1996) *The Changing Nature of Irish Voluntary Social Service Organisations,* School of Business Studies, Trinity College, Dublin.

Johnson, N. (1987) *The Welfare State in Transition: The Theory and Practice of Welfare Pluralism*, Wheatstaff Press, Brighton.

Joyce, L. and McCashin, T. (1987) In *Poverty and Social Policy*, Institute of Public Administration, Dublin.

Keane, J. (1984) *Public Life and Late Capitalism*, Cambridge University Press, Cambridge.

Keane, J. (1988) *Democracy and Civil Society*, Verso, London.

Keenan, D. (1983) *The Catholic Church in Nineteenth Century Ireland*, Dublin.

Kendall, J. and Knapp, M. (1996) In Smith, J.D., Rochester, C. and Hedley, R. *An Introduction to the Voluntary Sector*, Routledge, London.

Kennedy, S. (1981) *Who Should Care? The Development of Kilkenny Social Services, 1963–1980*, Turoe Press, Dublin.

Kerr, D. (1982) *Peel, Priests and People*, Oxford University Press, Oxford.

Knapp, M. (1996) In Billis, D. and Harris, M. *Voluntary Agencies: Challenges of Organisation and Management*, Macmillan, London.

Knight, B. (1993) *Voluntary Action*, Home Office, London.

Knight, B. and Stokes, P. (1996) *The Deficit in Civil Society in the UK*, Foundation for Civil Society, Birmingham.

Kramer, R. (1981) *Voluntary Agencies in the Welfare State*, University of California Press, Berkeley, CA.

Kramer, R., Lorentzen, H., Melief, W. and Pasquinelli, S. (1993) *Privatization in Four European Countries: Comparative Studies in Government – Third sector Relationships*, M. E. Sharpe, New York.

Kramer, R. (1990) *Voluntary Organizations in the Welfare State: On the Threshold of the 90s*, The Centre for Voluntary Organisations, London.

Landry, C. and Mulgan, G. (1995) *The Other Invisible Hand: Remaking Charity for the 21st Century*, DEMOS, London.

Lansley, J. (1996) In Deakin, N. and Kershaw, J. *Selected Papers for the Report of the Commission on the Future of the Voluntary Sector*, NCVO, London.

Leat, D. (1990) *The Kaleidescope of Care: A Review of Research on Welfare Provision for Elderly People*, The National Institute for Social Work, London.

Leat, D. (1995) In Smith, J.D., Rochester, C. and Hedley, R. *An Introduction to the Voluntary Sector*, Routledge, London.

Lee, A. (1990) In *Community Work in Ireland: Trends in the 80's, Options for the 90's*, Combat Poverty Agency, Dublin.

Lee, P. and Raban, C. (1988) *Welfare Theory and Social Policy*, Sage, London.

Lichtheim, G. (1970) *A Short History of Socialism*, Fontana, London.

Lis, C. and Soly, H. (1979) *Poverty and Capitalism in Pre-Industrial Europe*, Harvester, Sussex.

Looney, M. (1986) *The Politics of Greed*, Pluto Press, London.

Malthus, T.R. (1798) *Essay on the Principles of Population*, London.

Marquand, D. (1996), Victorian Values, Modern Strife, *The Guardian*, 28 October.

Marshall, T. In Billis, D. And Harris, M. (1996) *Voluntary Agencies: Challenges of Organisation and Management*, Macmillan, London.

Marshall, T.H. (1973) *Class, Citizenship and Social Development*, Westport, CT.

Marsland, D. (1995) *Self Reliance*, Transaction Books, New Brunswick, NJ.

Marsland, D. (1996) *Welfare or Welfare State?* Macmillan, London.

Martin, M. (1994) *Virtuous Giving: Philanthropy, Voluntary Service and Caring*, Indiana University Press, Indianapolis, IN.

Maxwell, C. (1979) *Dublin Under the Georges*, Dublin.

McPherson, J.M. (1991) A Dynamic Model of Voluntary Affiliation, *Social Forces*, Vol. 59, No. 3, March.

McSweeney, A.M. (1917) *Poverty in Cork*, UCC, Cork.

Mishra, R. (1977) *Society and Social Policy*, Macmillian, London.

Mulvihill, R. (1995) *Voluntary-Statutory Partnership in Community Care of the Elderly*, National Council for the Elderly, Dublin.

Mulvihill, R., and Ruddle, H. (1995) *Charitable Giving and Volunteering in the Republic of Ireland*, Policy Research Centre, National College of Industrial Relations, Dublin.

Murray, C. (1984) *Losing Ground: American Social Policy 1950-1980*, Basic Books, New York.

Netherlands Platform for Welfare Affairs (1995) *White Paper on Social Policy and Everyday Practice*, PIN, Rijswijk.

O'Donovan, O. and Varley, T. (1995) *Voluntary Sector Employment: A Secondary Labour Market? A Review of the Literature*, Galway Social Sciences Research Centre, UCG, Galway.

O'Mahony, A. (1981) *Social Need and the Provision of Social Services in Rural Areas: A Case Study for the Community Care Services*, The Agricultural Institute, Dublin.

Offe, C. (1984) *Contradictions of the Welfare State*, Hutchinson, London.

O'Leary, J. (1954) Social Topics, *Christus Rex*, January/April.

Oliver, M. (1996) In *The Report of the Commission on the Future of the Voluntary Sector – Selected Papers*, National Council for Voluntary Organisations, London.

Papal Encyclical (1931) *Quadregesimo Anno*, Rome.

Parker, P. And Froland, C. (1983) Rediscovering Self-Help: Its Role in Social Care in *Social Service Policy Systems*, Volume 6, Sage Publications, California.

Pearce, J. (1993) *The Organizational Behavior of Unpaid Workers*, Routledge, London.

Peillon, M. (1995) Support for Welfare in Ireland, *Administration* 43 (3), Autumn.

Pelling, H. (1965) *The Origins of the Labour Party*, Oxford, Clarendon Press.

Petty, W. (1691) *Political Anatomy of Ireland*, London.

Phillips, M. (1997) Fallacies and Illusions of the Welfare State, *Times Literary Supplement*, 14 March.

Pierson, C. (1991) *Beyond the Welfare State?* Polity, Cambridge.

Piven, F.F. & Cloward, R. (1985) *The New Class War*, Random House, New

York.

Powell, F.W. (1992) *The Politics of Irish Social Policy*, Edwin Mellen Press, New York.

Putnam, R. (1993) *Making Democracy Work: Civic Traditions in Modern Italy*, Princeton University Press, Princeton, NJ.

Report of the Commission on the Future of the Voluntary Sector (1996) *Voluntary Action into the 21st Century*, National Council for Voluntary Organisations, London.

Reports of Dublin Mendicity Association, (1818–1828) Dublin.

Rice, R. (1992) Impact of Government Contracts on Voluntary Social Agencies in *Social Casework*, No. 56.

Rochester, C. (1995) In Smith, J.D., Rochester, C., Hedley, R. *An Introduction to the Voluntary Sector*, Routledge, London.

Ruddle, H. and Mulvihill, R. (1995) *Charitable Giving and Volunteering in the Republic of Ireland*, Policy Research Centre, National College of Industrial Relations, Dublin.

Ruddle, H. and O'Connor, J. (1993) *Reaching Out: Charitable Giving and Volunteering in the Republic of Ireland*, National College of Industrial Relations, Dublin.

Rusche, G. and Kirchheimer, O. (1939) *Punishment and Social Structure*, Columbia University Press, New York.

Sabel, C. (1996) *Ireland: Local Partnership and Social Innovation*, OECD, Paris.

Salamon, L. (1994) *The Global Association Revolution*, DEMOS, London.

Seligman, A.B. (1996) Animad Versions on Civil Society & Civic Virtue in J. A. Hall (ed.), *Civil Society*, Polity Cambridge.

Shaw, G.B. (1896) *Report on Fabian Theory*, Fabian Tract No. 70, Fabian Society, London.

Smith, D., Baldwin, D. and White, E., in Tip Connors (1988) *The Non Profit Organisation Handbook*, McGraw-Hill, New York.

Smith, J.D., (1996) In Billis, D. and Harris, M. *Voluntary Agencies: Challenges of Organisation and Management*, Macmillan, London.

Spicer, P. (1988) *Principles of Social Welfare: An Introduction to the Welfare State*, Routledge, London.

Squires, P. (1990) *Anti Social Policy*, Polity, Oxford.

Starkey, T. (1533) *A Dialogue between Reginald Pole and Thomas Lipset* (ed. K.M. Burton, 1948), London.

Starrat, M. (1832) *History of Ancient & Modern Dublin*, Dublin.

Stokes, P. and Knight, B. (1997) A Citizens' Charter to Save our Cities, *Independent*, 1 January.

Taylor, M. (1996) In Deakin, N. and Kershaw, J. *Selected Papers for the Report of the Commission on the Future of the Voluntary Sector*, NCVO, London.

Teeple, G. (1995) *Globalization and the Decline of Social Reform*, Garamond Press, Toronto.

Titmuss, R. (1970) *The Gift Relationship*, Allen & Unwin, London.

Twine, F. (1994) *Citizenship and Social Rights*, Sage, London.

Walzer, M. (1983) *Spheres of Justice: A Defence of Pluralism*, Robertson, Oxford.

Webb, A. and Wistow, G. (1986) *Planning Need and Scarcity*, Allen & Unwin, London.

Webb, B. (1926) *My Apprenticeship*, London.

Webb, B. (1948) *Our Partnership*, London.

Wedel, J. (ed.) (1992) In *Unplanned Society: Poland during and after Communism*, Columbia University Press, New York.

Wedel, J. (1994) US aid to Central and Eastern Europe in *East-Central Europe Economies in Transition*, Congress of the United States, US Government Printing Office, Washington.

Whateley, R. (1836) *Royal Commission on Poorer Classes*, Vol. XXX, London.

Wolfenden Committee (1978) *The Future of Voluntary Organisations*, Croom Helm, London.

Woodroofe, K. (1962) *From Charity to Social Work*, Routledge and Kegan Paul, London.

WRAC (1993) *Labour Market Policy and Long-term Unemployment*, National Economic and Social Forum, Dublin.

Index

active citizenship, 16, 19, 21, 22, 30, 48, 84, 89, 148
Adam Ferguson, 12
ADM, 157
Advisory Group on Charities/Fund-raising Legislation, 1996, 163
Alexis de Tocqueville, 12
altruism, 16, 17, 24, 30, 35, 36, 92, 94, 98, 145
Anderson, 14
Antonio Gramsci, 13
Antonio Rosmini-Serbati, 34
Aristotle, 19

Beck, 86, 87
beneficence, 47, 65, 92, 112
Berking, 16
Better Local Government - A Programme for Change (1996), 147
Billis, 113, 126
Booth, 37
Borrie Report, 21
Bradshaw, 66
Breen, 105
Brenton, 105, 146, 157
Bulmer, 92, 126
bureaucracy, 22, 126, 138, 158
Butler, 137

capitalist, 41, 42, 43, 78
Carmen, 17
Catholic, 17, 33, 34, 37, 38, 65, 66, 72, 73, 74, 75, 80, 113, 115, 121, 135
CE, 60, 61, 127, 128, 130, 132, 158
charity, 16, 34, 65, 66, 67, 68, 69, 70, 73, 91, 121, 152, 153, 163
Charles I, 66
Chopko, 23
Christianity, 16
citizen, 15, 16, 18, 20, 22, 24, 45, 52, 53, 61, 84, 101, 115, 137
civic association, 22
Civic Forum Movement, 23
Cloward, 37, 60
Cloward and Piven, 37
Coakley, 58
Cohen, 15, 16, 55
Cohen and Arato, 15, 16
Cole and Postgate, 35, 43
collectivism, 18, 19, 20, 21, 36
Combat Poverty Agency, 54
Comité des Sages, 25, 26, 48
communication, 15, 17, 88, 143, 159, 160
Communitarianism, 76
Community Employment, 60, 61, 127, 129
Conference of Major Religious Superiors, 63, 64

conservatism, 11
Corkery, 78
Corporatist, 53
Costello Report, 148, 162
Cousins, 98
Crickley and Devlin, 81, 104
Croft and Beresford, 166
Culpitt, 47, 48, 145
Curry, 102, 137
Curtis, 120

Dahl, 165
Dahrendorf, 25, 55
Danube Circle, 23
Darvil and Mundy, 126, 127
Davis, 56, 120, 168
De Swann, 38, 65, 66, 91
Dean, 67
democracy, 11, 12, 44, 45, 47, 52,
    63, 78, 84, 85, 89, 109, 126, 138,
    165, 166
Democratic Programme, 79
dependency, 20, 39, 57, 59, 82
Dept. of Social Welfare, 133, 134,
    161
Dobbs, 67
Donzelot, 65
Dublin Mendicity Association, 69,
    70, 71, 72

Eamonn de Valera, 38
Ecological Movement, 88
Elizabeth I, 66
empowerment, 22, 29, 31, 89,
    109, 170, 174
Enlightenment, 12, 45
Erskine Childers, 114
Esping Andersen, 52

ESRI, 54
Etzioni, 21, 22, 82, 89
EU, 134, 135, 138, 144, 147, 154,
    161, 175

Fabian, 20, 32, 33, 34, 37, 39, 41
family, 12, 15, 18, 21, 22, 30, 43,
    51, 62, 74, 84, 87, 114, 121
FAS, 127, 128, 130
Faughnan, 101, 113, 116, 135,
    136, 140, 156, 158, 159, 169
Faughan and Kelleher, 76
feminist, 26, 45
Fianna Fáil, 80
Forde, 81
Fr. Jerome O'Leary, 74
Freeman's Journal, 72
Fukuyuma, 17, 21, 22, 95, 165

Gaskin and Smith, 28, 114, 115,
    116
Gay Rights movement, 82
George and Wildings, 41
George Soros, 14
Gerard, 92
Giddens, 86, 109
Gladstone, 91, 157
Goodin, 57
Green Paper on Social Policy, 51
Green Paper on the Voluntary
    and Community Sector, 24

H. G. Wells, 33
Habermas, 15, 44
Hann and Dunn, 13, 14
Harvey, 148, 159
Hatch, 157
Havel, 14

Hayek, 18, 39

Health Act, 1953, 136, 161
Healy, 56, 64
Hedley and Smith, 121
Hegel, 12
Henry George, 33, 34

Ignatieff, 46
Inglis, 72
Irish Council for Social Housing,
   137
Irish Council for Social Welfare,
   133
Irish Times, 44, 56, 64, 75

Jaffro, 133, 134
James Connolly, 79
John Locke, 11
Johnson, 144, 145

Keane, 11, 22, 44
Keenan, 73
Kendall and Knapp, 94
Kerr, 73
Knapp, 94, 156
Knight, 16, 29, 98, 99, 104
Kramer, 24, 29, 96, 107, 126, 146,
   156, 157

Labour Movement, 79
laissez-faire capitalism, 40
Landry and Mulgan, 22, 105
Lansley, 166, 168
Leat, 125, 148, 163, 164
Lee and Raban, 42, 43, 44
Leibniz, 66
lifeworld, 15

Lis and Soly, 67

Looney, 92

Machiavelli, 32
MacPherson, 120
Malthus, 67

Marquand, 19, 20
Marshall, 52, 96, 97
Marsland, 18, 39
Martin, 152
Marx, 13, 42, 43
Marxist, 13, 33, 41, 44
Mary Daly, 45
Maxwell, 68
McCashin and Joyce, 113
Melanie Phillips, 45
Michael Davitt, 34
Mill, 35
Mishra, 36, 41, 145
Mitterand, 23
Modernisation, 77, 80
modernity, 17, 33, 77, 85, 86,
   101, 105
Montesquieu, 19
Muintir na Tire, 80, 81, 82, 113
Mulgan and Landry, 101
Murray, 18, 39, 47
Mutual aid, 78

National Lottery, 139, 140, 148,
   149, 150, 151, 152, 155, 175
National Social Service Council,
   137
National Social Services Board,
   24, 137
National, Economic and Social

Forum, 128
Nazi, 24, 36, 62
New Deal, 37, 43, 59
New Right, 38, 57, 92
Northern Ireland, 24, 26, 27
NSSB, 99, 100, 137

O'Donovan and Varley, 98, 127
O'Mahony, 99, 157
Observer, 40, 59
OECD, 137, 138, 157
Offe, 43
Oliver, 104

Parker and Froland, 171
partnership, 9, 25, 26, 27, 31, 34,
    51, 53, 81, 83, 89, 90, 91, 134,
    135, 137, 138, 144, 147, 154,
    161, 170, 175
Partnership 2000, 27, 51, 53
Pearce, 92, 94
Peillon, 26, 27
philanthropy, 65
Pierson, 44
Plato, 32
Poor Law, 34, 60, 63, 72
Pope Pius XI, 73
poverty, 27, 33, 35, 36, 39, 50, 51,
    54, 56, 57, 58, 63, 65, 77, 98
President Clinton, 59
President Mary Robinson, 113
privatisation, 15, 144, 145
professionalization, 29
*Programme for Competitiveness
    and Work*, 53
Programme for National Recovery,
    53
Putnam, 17, 22, 166

Quadragesima Anno, 73

Reflexive modernity, 86
Regan, 23, 75
*Report of the Commission on the
    Future of the Voluntary Sector*,
    25, 28, 29, 98, 160
Rice, 106
Robert Owen, 13, 78
Rochester, 148, 163, 164
Rowntree, 37
Ruddle and Mulvihill, 119, 120,
    162
Ruddle and O'Connor, 28, 153
Ruddle and Donoghue, 107, 122
Rusche and Kirchheimer, 66

Saint-Simon, Fourier and Cabet,,
13
Salamon, 23
Salamon and Anheier, 96
Scruton, 40
secondary labour market, 60,
    127, 128, 132, 175
Seligman, 33
Shaw, 33
Smith, 28, 37, 98, 107, 114, 115,
    116, 120, 121, 168
social capital, 21
Social Chapter, 83
social exclusion, 50, 51, 54, 55,
    58, 60, 62
social fragmentation, 25
socialist, 34, 41, 42, 52, 78, 115
solidarity, 15, 16, 18, 23, 50, 54,
    64, 83, 92, 99, 112, 170
solidary individualism, 16, 20,

21, 30
Spicer, 91, 92
Sr. Stanislaus Kennedy, 136
Stokes and Knight, 16
Subsidiarity, 72, 135
Sweden, 28, 36, 107, 114, 115, 116, 121

Taylor, 125, 166, 170
Teeple, 19
Tenants Leagues, 79, 80
Thatcherism, 20
The Green Paper on the Community and Voluntary Sector, 50, 74, 82, 84, 89
Theodicy, 65, 67
Thomas Davidson, 34
Thomas Hobbes, 12
Thomas Paine, 12
Thomas Starkey, 33
Titmuss, 34
Tonnies, 76
Travelling community, 25
trust, 16, 17, 21, 22, 30, 48, 49, 50, 56, 61, 63, 72, 75, 91, 94
Twine, 58, 62

U.N, 81
Underclass, 54
unemployment, 43, 44, 51, 54, 55, 59, 60, 79, 83, 128

Victorian, 20, 36, 57
Voluntarism, 24, 50, 58, 65, 89, 91, 113
volunteer, 27, 28, 29, 61, 93, 94, 95, 111, 113, 117, 119, 120, 121, 125, 131, 153, 154, 162, 174

Walzer, 19
Waters, 44
Webb, 33, 34, 37
Webb and Wistow, 146
Wedel, 11
welfare pluralism, 47, 89, 134, 135, 154, 157, 175
Welfare State, 11, 16, 18, 20, 21, 22, 23, 25, 26, 27, 30, 36, 37, 38, 39, 41, 43, 44, 45, 46, 47, 48, 52, 53, 57, 58, 59, 62, 82, 83, 89, 91
Whateley, 69, 70
William Petty, 67
William Thompson, 13, 35, 78
Wolfenden Report, 158
Women's Movement, 79, 88
Woodroofe, 69
workfare, 49, 51, 58, 59, 60, 61, 62, 64, 132, 175